D0999955

DYNAMICS OF CHARACTER

DYNAMICS OF CHARACTER

Self-Regulation in Psychopathology

DAVID SHAPIRO

BASIC
BOOKS
A Member of the Perseus Books Group

Library of Congress Cataloging-in-Publication Data
Shapiro, David, 1926–
    Dynamics of character : self-regulation in psychopathology / David Shapiro.
        p.   cm.
    Includes bibliographical references and index.
    ISBN 0-465-09571-2
    1. Temperament.   2. Psychology, Pathological.   3. Character.   4. Will.   5. Schizophrenia.
I. Title.
RC455.5.T45.S46   1999
616.89—dc21   99-04869
                                                                                                          CIP

00   01   02   03   /   10   9   8   7   6   5   4   3   2   1

In memory of my brother,
Arthur Shapiro

Contents

Acknowledgments

I would like once again to express my gratitude to my friend Dr. Jean Schimek for his critical reading of the manuscript in the face of my own impatience. I have been fortunate, also, to have the assistance of Mustafa Atakay, Murat Paker, M.D., and Michael Jackson during various phases of the writing and preparation of the book and I wish to thank each of them for their valuable help. My editor, Cindy Hyden, of Basic Books has been exceedingly helpful in the book's preparation, and I appreciate her work. Finally, I want to thank my wife, Gerry Shapiro, whose advice on innumerable matters in the course of writing has as usual been indispensable.

Some parts of Chapters 1 and 2 have appeared in different form in the journal *Social Research*, and I am grateful for permission to use that material here.

Preface

For some time I have wanted to extend and also deepen my earlier studies of psychopathology, all the more now in light of the current challenge to psychological understanding from biological science. My earlier work on neurotic styles attempts to describe quite closely the formal qualities of various kinds of neurotic experience and behavior, such as the ways of thinking, the attitudes (particularly the unrecognized attitudes), and the modes of action that characterize the different neurotic conditions. I was interested in the description and analysis of the general forms of pathological experience and behavior because these forms or styles seemed to constitute what might be called the structure of the pathological character and, in turn, determined the form of characteristic symptoms.

The study of the ways the mind works, of what Wilhelm Reich called "ways of being," necessarily leads to a different perception of the dynamics of psychopathology from the traditional psychoanalytic one. It leads to a picture of a consciously purposeful individual whose activity and the attitudes that shape it are not mere products of the pathological dynamics but are central to those dynamics. It is a more inclusive dynamics, one that includes the defensive function of the individual style of cognition and action, the subjective forms of motivation, and the qualities of conscious experience in general. This dynamics of the whole character is, in my opinion, a view of the individual's self-regulation that is sounder theoretically and more useful therapeutically than the traditional dynamics of drive-defense conflicts. In particular, it opens the door to a better understanding of the subjective necessity of the forms that symptoms take.

One of the unexpected products of my earlier work was the suggestion of certain formal relations or kinships between kinds of psychopathology that were symptomatically quite disparate, such as between obsessional and paranoid conditions. Further formal analysis, I have thought, might permit an understanding of psychopathology in terms of still more fundamental dimensions and a clearer picture of the relations of the various kinds of psychopathology to one another, and also of dynamic processes common to them.

In particular, I have long been impressed with the fact that the symptomatic behavior of all the different kinds of psychopathology is characterized clinically either by a comparatively unreflective, spur-of-the-moment planlessness, on the one hand, or rigidity, direction by fixed internal rules, on the other. Both of these are modes of activity that entail a diminished volitional experience. That is, they entail a diminished experience of self-direction (as in decision), or personal responsibility, or agency. It is not hard to see the defensive or anxiety-forestalling value of such modes of action.

My interest in more fundamental dimensions of psychopathology has been focused especially on that idea, on determining whether the various forms of psychopathology can be understood as varieties of general modes of diminished agency. It is not my aim to reduce all the kinds of psychopathology and the kinds of character from which symptoms arise to a single model. It is, rather, to understand the relations among them and in that way to understand what means of self-regulation they may share.

The fact that we are able to perceive formal relations and kinships among conditions of extremely diverse symptoms, perhaps even across the gap that separates psychotic from neurotic symptoms, has another, more immediate, value. It seems to me a refutation of the idea of diverse, specific causes for those conditions, whether that idea be of particular childhood conflicts or traumas, as so commonly thought in the past, or particular biological defects, so popular at present. The study of the formal structures of psychopathology can, in other words, restrain the temptation, to which our scientifically still-immature field is so susceptible, to find causes that are too simple for complicated conditions.

SECTION ONE
STRUCTURE AND DYNAMICS

CHAPTER ONE

Introduction

This book is written against the current. The medicalization of psychiatry is increasingly apparent, and interest in psychopathology has turned for the moment toward biology. The trend includes a diminished interest in the psychology of psychopathology altogether, but it particularly involves a diminished psychoanalytic influence. One would not have predicted this development thirty or forty years ago. After World War II, psychoanalytic understanding was ascendant in psychiatry, at least intellectually, and its influence was critical in the rapid development of clinical psychology and probably clinical social work as well. Psychoanalysis offered a comprehensive psychological theory of psychopathology, particularly of neurosis. It was, in fact, the only comprehensive and detailed theory in existence. The fact is, if one includes its contemporary modifications, it remains so; it has not been superseded, at least by any other psychological theory. It is therefore all the more striking that psychoanalytic influence has waned in its primary field of discovery. I do not think that this development can be attributed entirely to the advances in neuroscience, or to the effectiveness of pharmacological treatment of some kinds of mental illness. It must be taken, also, as an expression of dissatisfaction and disappointment with the theory itself, and for that matter with psychological theory altogether in this field.

Biological explanation of psychopathology, for its part, is often simplistic. The identification of particular biological processes that may be involved in a condition cannot explain the volitional behavior, the cognitive processes, and the ideational and affective content that ultimately constitute the condition.

For example, certain physiological conditions have been identified that can explain various effects of self-administered opiates and may provide an incentive for their use. But these conditions constitute only "a permissive substrate" for drug abuse (Cacioppo and Berntson, 1992). The frame of mind, the evaluation of circumstances, and the decisions and actions required for actual drug abuse involve much more than the existence of an incentive. An incentive may be sufficient explanation for the behavior of a rat but, in humans, incentive can account only for temptation. One can no more explain drug abuse by an incentive of this kind than one can explain an act of rape by a high level of testosterone. Such actions, or any human actions of consequence, require a far more complex coalition of neurophysiological processes than have so far been discovered. In fact, it follows from such considerations that explanation on a psychological level is not only essential but will probably be essential, also, for pointing out directions for further neurophysiological discovery.

No one doubts that psychopathology, or, for that matter, the possibilities of human psychology in general, is founded on human biology. We are able to think, to talk, on account of our biology. We owe to our brain, in fact, our capacity for self-awareness and, with that, our susceptibility to internal conflict and self-deception. Everyone understands, also, that individual biological variations influence individual psychology, and do so from the beginning of life. But the predominant effort of the present trend in psychiatry has been to locate specific neurophysiological causes for complex psychological symptoms, circumventing the psychological foundation of those symptoms. The failure to establish such specific neurophysiological causes for specific symptoms has not yet discouraged that effort.

The presumption of a specific neurophysiological cause of obsessive-compulsive conditions is a conspicuous example. A popular book on these conditions (Rapoport, 1989), written by a scientist, speculates, for instance, on the possibility of a relation between compulsive hand washing and the presumably innate, neurologically determined grooming rituals of some primates. Even cursory psychological investigation, I believe, will refute such a view. It will show that compulsive hand washing is not a mindless or reflexive reaction, but action aimed at dispelling a particular, relentless kind of anxiety, an anxiety regularly characterized by a certain type of content. In my own clinical experience and that of many others, furthermore, the symptom of compulsive hand washing is regularly associated with other compulsive symptoms, such as precautionary checking and rechecking that the door is locked, the oven turned off, and so on, or with obsessional symptoms, such as agonizing indecision. All these symptoms reflect, as I shall describe in more detail later, a special and peculiar kind of conscientiousness. Such symptoms are, in other words, expressions of psychological dynamics and products of certain attitudes and ways of thinking. They are reflections of a kind of character or a kind of mind, not discrete diseases unrelated to personality or mind.

Human biology is the foundation not only of the capacity for language and thought and self-awareness but, also, for human relationships. It determines that children will be raised by adults, that this upbringing will be lengthy, and that it will take place almost surely in societies of one sort or another. And all this implies, given human cognitive and emotional capacities, the possibility of the development of such peculiarly conscientious attitudes as those I just alluded to, whose product, in turn, is obsessive-compulsive symptoms.

Psychoanalysis, in its traditional form, is not very well placed to answer simplistic biological notions of psychopathology with satisfactory alternatives. The reason for this lies in the limitations of its understanding of symptom formation, specifically in its failure to explain the form of symptoms, why a symptom is of this type rather than of that type. This deficiency, in turn, is a direct result of its historically insufficient recognition of the significance of the attitudes, the individual ways of thinking and modes of activity, the "forms of the mind" that shape consciousness and behavior.

Early psychoanalysis saw neurotic symptoms as particular irrationalities in an otherwise rational adult. It explained them as expressions of particular childhood conflicts, unconsciously preserved anachronisms. Now, however, most symptoms are recognized by analysts and therapists as more characterological, at least in the somewhat vague sense of consisting of fairly general features of attitude, behavior, or relationships. But this clinical view has not been accompanied by conceptual clarity and, probably as a consequence, it is far from complete. A convincing understanding of symptoms must recognize that their dynamics, whatever their origin, are no longer contained in particular conflicts stored in memory, or in particular, largely ideational representations of such conflicts. The dynamics of the adult's pathology consists of the ways in which the adult character organization works.

This book will continue my earlier work toward a characterological understanding of psychopathology. Although that understanding is different from the traditional psychoanalytic picture, it is derived from the psychoanalytic conception of the mind's structure. It aims at a picture of the ways the mind is organized and the ways in which it organizes experience and regulates itself, in the various forms of psychopathology. This is a picture of the individual's attitudes, of the organization and dynamics of those attitudes, including those attitudes of which he is not aware and of which he would not be able to articulate. At the same time it is a picture of the modes of activity and kinds of reaction associated with those attitudes.

When psychopathology is studied in this way, it appears in a new light. Quite disparate-seeming symptoms and behavioral traits often reveal themselves to be variations, sometimes rather slight variations, of more general modes and ways of being. Relations of a formal kind appear between seemingly unrelated diagnostic categories. Thus it may be possible to understand the varieties of psychopathology, with their enormously diverse symptoms, as variations of the mind's organizing and regulating system. This structural or characterological understanding, therefore, points in exactly the opposite direction from the current psychiatric aim of establishing specific neurophysiological causes for discrete conditions.

THE PSYCHOANALYTIC EGO

To a diligent student the body of psychoanalytic theory of psychopathology can only be daunting. It is exceedingly complicated, in places so tangled as to be almost impenetrable. The reason for these complications is respectable enough. They are largely the accumulated products of an extended period of clinical observation and discovery, the new being added to the old, seldom replacing it.

Freud's earliest theory was simplicity itself. His search was for specific causes for particular symptoms, a tic, say, or a particular phobia. He found such causes, or believed he found them, in the repressed memories of traumatic events and their dammed-up affects. In this picture of psychopathology there was almost no suggestion of the mind's general structure, the organization that produced and gave form to the symptoms. The important exception, of course, was the critical concept of defense, in the simplest sense of repression; it was the mind's self-protective device. But otherwise, the symptom and the pathology had little to do with the individual personality or organization of the mind and much to do with the memory of particular events that, it was thought, had lodged in the mind.

With Freud's subsequent shift to the theory of libidinal development and its idea of intrinsically developmental conflict, the picture of psychopathology became far more comprehensive. It also became, as the picture of the mind itself became, far more complicated. For this reason, from that time forward, as the fabric of neurosis continued to unfold in clinical work and more and more of the personality was seen to be involved, psychoanalytic therapy became longer and longer. The theory of psychopathology was necessarily enlarged to include these additional constituents and processes of the personality. For example, while originally the process of defense—the anxiety-forestalling restriction of self-awareness—consisted simply of repression, further clinical experience indicated various additional anxiety-forestalling processes, and the list of the recognized defense "mechanisms" grew.

The systematization of these developments was an aim and to a certain extent an accomplishment of Freud's introduction in 1923 of an explicitly structural picture of the mind. That aim is succinctly conveyed in his definition, at the time, of the ego, the central structural concept, as "a coherent organization of mental processes," and the particularly interesting addendum to that definition in which he said that "it is the mental agency which supervises all its own constituent processes" (Freud, 1923/1961, p. 17).

But in actual fact the development of the conception of the ego since then has not been of "a coherent organization of mental processes." Instead, the ego has simply been credited with an unsystematic accumulation of functions, processes, and mechanisms as clinical evidence from time to time suggested or theory seemed to require. Some years ago the eminent psychoanalyst Robert Waelder described the list of defense mechanisms that was more or less standard at the time as "a haphazard collection" (Waelder, 1960). Consider, for example, the defense mechanisms that are generally associated with obsessive-compulsive neurosis: reaction-formation, intellectualization, isolation of affect, undoing, and regression. These mechanisms are overlapping, of markedly different levels of complexity, at various conceptual distances from clinical observation, and without any systematic relation to one another. Nor has the list of defense mechanisms become less haphazard with the more recent addition of those associated with the severe, though nonpsychotic, borderline conditions.

I believe it is fair to describe not only the list of defense mechanisms but the present psychoanalytic conception of the ego altogether as a haphazard collection, in this case including not only the defense mechanisms but, also, various adaptive capacities and ideational contents, all without clear relation to one another or overall organization. In short, as the ego is presently conceived, it is, as Einstein remarked of the state of particle physics, less a system than a catalog. As a consequence, individuals are often described and their pathology explained, in psychoanalytic discussion, with ad hoc constructions of a kind that can only be likened to Rube Goldberg contraptions.

THE MIND'S STRUCTURE AND DYNAMICS

The mind is not only a coherent organization; it is, also, an organizer. Our subjective life is organized by attitudes and ways of thinking that are characteristic of each of us. These characteristic attitudes function, also, as a regulatory system. They automatically, reflexively, limit or correct propensities or reactions, perhaps to special circumstances, that might threaten the individual's stability or a present adaptation, even if that stability or adaptation is a pathological one. A guarded person, say, who is tempted in special circumstances to relax his guard, is likely to notice something suspect in time to annul that temptation. It is the attitude of guardedness itself that translates the sensation of that incipient relaxation into an experience of vulnerability and thereby triggers a corrective reassertion of alertness.

The conception of the mind's structure, or the person's character, as a self-regulating system implies a new picture of psychological dynamics. It is a picture that especially revises our view of the role of consciousness in the dynamics of psychopathology. In the traditional psychoanalytic view, consciousness was largely irrelevant to the dynamics of psychopathology, an epiphenomenon registering the effects of unconscious processes. It was a view that was consistent with the nineteenth-century passive-associationist conception of the mind. But we now recognize consciousness as itself an active organizer of experience.

That recognition places characteristic attitudes of consciousness, including attitudes of which the individual may be largely or wholly unaware but that shape his subjective experience, in a central dynamic role. In particular, the restrictive workings of those attitudes, by limiting or distorting self-awareness in ways that forestall anxiety, effectively constitute the processes of defense. From this standpoint, therefore, the psychoanalytic mechanisms of defense can be seen as special, on the whole clinically conspicuous, instances of the working of this regulatory system. These mechanisms can be seen not as mental devices "used" by the individual but as instances of the way the individual's mind works.

The mind's organizing and regulatory system can be described as its "structure" in much the same sense that the architect uses that term. The building's structure is what holds it up; in doing so it gives the building its essential form. The mind's structure or character is, correspondingly, the system of attitudes and ways that not only guarantees comparative stability and comfort in a wide variety of circumstances but, also, in doing so, gives individual function consistency and determines its general forms.

The architecture of certain kinds of character, however, gives rise to psychopathology. Character has developed in ways that forestall conflict and instability only by severe and continuing restrictions of subjective life and behavior. In these cases, in other words, the individual has reacted restrictively against certain of his own tendencies—his own feelings, ideas, intentions, even certain of his own attitudes. That very restrictiveness, aimed to forestall anxiety, creates conditions that generate new anxiety. For example, the carefully controlled, guarded person is no longer discomforted only by the circumstances or conflict originally responsible for his guardedness; once guarded, he is discomforted by the smallest surprise or briefest spontaneity. And each such discomfort prompts a reinforcement of his guardedness. Character restrictions of this sort, by tightening the limits of expression, not only create tension but also broaden the area of conflict and the potential for anxiety.

Thus, in this circularity, the tense restrictions of character are continually reinforced, and the pathological character perpetuates itself. Special extensions and ramifications of these restrictive aspects of character often emerge and become conspicuous, and these, like compulsive hand washing, constitute the familiar psychiatric symptoms. Such symptoms will, therefore, invariably be "in character."

A great deal of clinical evidence confirms that the symptoms of psychopathology are, in fact, characterological. The man who is obsessed by an old regret that he himself calls "crazy" is driven also in his daily life by concerns that he might miss an opportunity and by his general perfectionism; he does not recognize these as symptoms, but they are strikingly similar in their subjective experience and the attitudes they reflect to the symptom that he does recognize. The Rorschach expert can often infer the existence of certain symptoms from the general manner in which his subject reacts to inkblots; considering the hysteric's impetuous reactiveness to the Rorschach cards, for example, he is not surprised by the emotional outbursts that she herself says "come from nowhere!"

We now know, in other words, that even the most peculiar symptoms, symptoms that seem strange to the person afflicted with them, are not the alien intrusions into everyday subjective life that they were once thought to be. They are, instead, special expressions of that subjective life, and of the kinds of attitudes that characterize it generally. It is in this specific sense that symptoms can be described as characterological, bearing in mind, again, the critical proviso that that subjective life and those characteristic attitudes are by no means necessarily consciously recognized or articulated. Neurotic symptoms feel strange or alien, when they do, not because they are intrusions of unconscious elements into everyday subjective life, but because they are conspicuous and troublesome extensions or ramifications of whole aspects of that subjective life that, despite their constant presence, are not consciously recognized.

Consider again, for example, the symptom of ritualistic, compulsive hand washing. This symptom typically emerges, as I said, in individuals more or less constantly nagged by a peculiarly relentless conscientiousness. These people constantly and uneasily remind themselves of something not done or not done enough; they cannot allow themselves to be satisfied. Consequently, they are often engaged in some corrective or precautionary action. They often do more to dispel or forestall their concern that they have not done enough. This kind of action, action done for the sake of having done it, is essentially ritualistic action. Until it becomes quite conspicuous, however, it is usually not recognized, at least by its subject, as symptomatic.

Quite small variations of a general attitude, such as an obsessively conscientious or dutiful attitude, can result in symptoms or traits that are superficially widely dissimilar. For example, in some individuals that attitude is expressed in a moralistic emphasis on "willpower," a distaste for self-indulgence or "giving in" to oneself. A slight variation of the same attitude is expressed in others in a drivenness in work. Sometimes an obsessive conscientiousness takes the form of relentless worrying; in a slightly different context of character, the symptom is a relentless perfectionism. In yet another person, unable to satisfy himself that his hands are clean, or clean enough, that attitude, or one very close to it, will have the result of compulsive hand washing.

It is evident, also, that the psychoanalytic defense mechanisms of reaction-formation and undoing are actually variants of this obsessively precautionary or corrective attitude. In these instances, that attitude is expressed in a precautionary or compensatory overcorrection, in the one case to forestall, in the other to dispel, anxiety over any possibility of wrongdoing.

When the characterological structure of various kinds of psychopathology emerges, relations and affinities among conditions with altogether different diagnoses also become apparent. These are formal relations, relations of quite general attitudes and forms of thinking and experience, which may not be at all evident in the specific content of the symptom or the descriptions of the defense mechanisms. Sometimes these formal relations confirm or extend relations already recognized by psychoanalysis on different grounds, but new relations or new aspects of familiar ones appear as well.

The relation between obsessive-compulsive and paranoid conditions is an interesting example. The obsessive fastidiousness or perfectionism that finds a blemish in everything is far removed, in the subject of its concern, from paranoid suspiciousness. But from the standpoint of cognitive attitude, and, for that matter, from the standpoint of the quality of subjective sensation, there is a striking likeness between the two. The tense purposefulness of each, the narrow concentration on the object of concern, the dismissal of its context and the consequently disproportionate estimate of its significance are all, not identical, but surely closely similar. And, in fact, the existence of a structural affinity is substantiated in those occasional cases where an anxious obsessive concern with, say, the possibility of dirt or contamination in food is intensified and elaborated to a concern with the possibility of poisoning.

A close relation between the two conditions has long been known to clinicians on simple empirical grounds. Severe obsessional pathology is a common background for paranoia, and in certain cases a differential diagnosis between the two is difficult to establish. Psychoanalysis has recognized the relation and explained it theoretically by the proximity of their presumed respective stages of fixation and regression, in both cases stages of anal libidinal and aggressive conflict. The theory did, therefore, recognize an intrinsic affinity between the two conditions, although on too narrow a basis. On the other hand, the defense mechanisms considered to be characteristic of each of the two conditions, those I mentioned earlier for the obsessive-compulsive and the mechanism of projection for paranoia, give no hint of their actual relation or the relation of the two kinds of character. The reason is clear. These defense mechanisms are not conceived as special expressions of the workings of obsessive-compulsive and paranoid characters, but as more or less elementary mental devices with only the most tenuous relation, if any, to the character in which they are found.

The defense mechanism of projection, in particular, is generally accepted as just such an elementary process of the mind. A consideration of the thought processes and attitudes involved in that mechanism, however, clarifies both its own workings and its close relation to the dynamics of obsessive-compulsive character. One only has to imagine a less stable and therefore more rigid transformation of the self-conscious self-control of a certain type of obsessive-compulsive character to obtain a glimpse of paranoid defensive concerns. The obsessive-compulsive person's concerns with self-control, his exaggerated efforts to forestall or repair any lapse of self-control (as in the defense mechanisms of reaction-formation and undoing), his constant wrestling with himself, and his concerns with weakness of will or giving in to himself—all this is transformed in the paranoid case into a defensive mobilization against giving in to an external agency that aims to overpower or weaken that will. It is this defensive mobilization, with its biased alertness, that finally results in "projective" distortions of reality. Thus a comparatively simple structural transformation, although obviously a significant one, results in a marked difference in the content of symptoms and defense processes.

Comparable relations can be found among other varieties of psychopathology. For example, there are close affinities of general style and subjective experience among various kinds of passive and impulsive character and between those and the highly emotional hysterical character. All of these conditions are characterized by an immediacy of reactiveness and a subjective sense of diminished intentionality ("I couldn't help it"; "I don't know why, I just did it"; "I'm ruled by my emotions"). Here, too, relatively small differences, say, in ways of thinking or in degree of immediacy of reaction, can account for significant variations in symptoms: volatile emotionality in one case; reckless action in another. There are interesting relations, also, between the driven spontaneity of hypomanic conditions, on the one hand, and both the drivenness of the compulsive and the impulsiveness of the psychopath. Both these relations have been noted separately and are mentioned in the clinical literature, particularly in the psychoanalytic literature, as has that between the hysterical character and the psychopath, but without the formal analysis that is necessary to clarify them.

If one could imagine a mind without structure, without an organizing and regulatory system, a mind that would be completely passive in its registration of circumstances and completely plastic in its susceptibility to them, then one could conceive of kinds of psychopathology as diverse as the kinds of pathogenic circumstances. But if we assume the existence of an organizing and regulatory system of some sort from the beginning, then it follows that however diverse the pathogenic circumstances, there will not be an unlimited diversity of pathology. The development of psychopathology will be limited to those general directions offered by the structural fault lines of the mind, so to speak. I believe that clinical experience confirms this. Of course, there is no limit to individual variation. But there seem to be comparatively few fundamental forms of psychopathology and those fundamental kinds appear to have more in common than their diverse symptoms often suggest.

SELF-ESTRANGEMENT AND
THE LOSS OF AGENCY AND VOLITION

Psychopathology of all varieties is marked by self-estrangement. It is the inevitable consequence of the anxiety-forestalling restrictions of subjective life that are intrinsic to the dynamics of psychopathology. Hence neurotic patients in psychotherapy regularly say such things as, "Why do I do it?"; "I want to move out, but somehow I don't"; "I don't know what I want"; "I think I love her, but I'm not sure."

In all forms of psychopathology there is some loss of a clear sense of what one actually feels, wants, and even what one intends to do. And there is a loss, as well, of the sense that one has wanted and chosen to do what one does or has done. This diminished sense of agency (Schafer, 1976), as it is called, or personal responsibility (Kaiser, 1955/1965), or personal autonomy or self-direction (Shapiro, 1981), as it has also been called, is conspicuous in symptomatic behavior that feels strange and unaccountable to its subject, such as compulsive rituals, or, more radically, in paranoid delusions. But it is evident also in the ease with which some individuals disavow intention, saying with sincerity, "It just happened, I didn't mean to hurt her," or, "I keep seeing him, but I really don't want to; it's like an addiction." The loss or dilution of the sense of personal agency is not limited to particular symptoms or particular behavior. It might be said to define symptomatic behavior, but in one form or another it is more or less continuously present in psychopathology. And it is not only the subjective experience of agency that is diminished. The *subjective* loss of agency is associated with some *actual limitation or impairment* of volitional action.

It is not remarkable that this is so. Self-awareness and the sense of personal agency are most acute in the exercise or anticipation of volitional action. It is therefore also at those times that motivational conflict and its anxiety are most acute. Diluting or attenuating that sense of agency and thereby forestalling that anxiety is accomplished by curtailing the actual processes of volitional self-direction.

For example, certain people generally act on the spur of the moment; they avoid serious planning and reflection on the consequences of their actions and, in fact, seem to avoid an attitude of deliberateness in general. Their spur-of-the-moment action makes it possible, even easy, to disavow responsibility or serious intention precisely because the volitional process and therefore their experience of it are so foreshortened. In other people, people of rigid character, a constant inner reference to rules or "should's," a consciousness of the authority of these "shoulds," limits volitional direction and dilutes the experience of agency or choice in a different way.

It is possible, in fact, to describe all the forms of psychopathology as characterized by a special reliance on what might be called prevolitional modes of activity, rigid or passively reactive modes that originate early in development, anxiety-forestalling modes of diminished agency-experience. I will use the term "prevolitional" throughout this book to describe and refer to these modes and the attitudes associated with them, but I do not mean to imply that their employment in adult psychopathology constitutes regression. Although these modes have early origins and are superseded in development by more fully volitional self-direction, they never completely disappear. They remain available in the repertoire of all adults where, as a rule, they are adaptively modified. I do not mean to suggest, either, that these modes constitute in some special sense the basic or elementary modes of psychopathology. Indeed, they overlap too much to be discrete and elementary, and in their extreme forms in schizophrenia they converge; an extreme of rigid reactiveness becomes an extreme of passive reactiveness. They are, however, exemplary of general modes of activity in which normal processes of volitional self-direction and the normal experience of volition, or agency, or personal responsibility is curtailed and the experience of anxiety is accordingly forestalled.

ETIOLOGY, STRUCTURAL CONTINUITY, AND SCHIZOPHRENIA

At present we can say very little with confidence about the etiology of psychopathology, either with regard to particular types or in general. Indeed, the search for causes—some would say the preoccupation with causes (Sass, 1994)—has had its problems. The field historically has been prone to the discovery of oversimplified causes and sources, psychological as well as biological, of the various sorts of psychopathology. Specific sources and causes have been debated, with emphasis now on this source, now on that one, before the fundamental nature of the pathology was established. In recent years, for example, there has been an increased emphasis within psychoanalysis on presumed deficiencies in very early, "pre-Oedipal" development, particularly the earliest relationship with the mother, in connection with certain severe, though nonpsychotic disorders. This emphasis has occasioned debate as to the "Oedipal" or "pre-Oedipal" sources of such pathology. But there is no reliable evidence to support either position, and the definitions of the pathologies are themselves quite vague and ambiguous. It may well be that the conception of an adult pathology has sometimes been prejudiced by premature assumptions of one or another developmental or biological cause.

Any psychopathology presents a complicated picture, and it is not easy to distinguish what is fundamental from what is merely conspicuous. The much discussed condition of anorexia nervosa is a case in point. In view of the patients' preoccupation with dieting and weight, the condition is usually described as an eating disorder. Early psychoanalytic understanding of anorexia, seeking its pathogenic sources in infantile drive conflict, presumed an oral fixation. The symptom was interpreted as an unconscious rejection of oral impregnation. But dieting and a preoccupation with weight can express aims and attitudes of different kinds, and more recent views recognize in anorexia an obsessive, even fanatical perfectionism and asceticism. This more characterological understanding naturally turns etiological interest in a different direction.

The psychoanalytic conception of development, and therefore also its view of psychopathology as a regressive phenomenon, is much broader now than its original picture of drive development and conflict. But to many clinicians, and I include myself, the traditional psychoanalytic identification of adult pathology with one or another stage of infant or child development, however broadly that stage may be understood, is mistaken in principle. Indeed, the invoking of the concept of regression itself, in this connection, without further explanation of the subjective processes presumably involved in it, seems questionable. It is extremely doubtful that the mentation of an early developmental stage actually can encompass the essential features of adult psychopathology. A childhood precursor of this or that adult trait, pathological or otherwise, can of course easily be found, but the distance between the childhood stage and the adult pathology remains very great, and if that distance is not recognized, the mind's development itself is slighted.

In the final analysis, the strongest reason for rejecting the identification of adult psychopathology with presumed prototypes in early childhood is the consistency of its symptoms with the adult character and its attitudes and modes. I have presented that clinical evidence elsewhere in some detail (Shapiro 1965, 1981) and I shall review some of it in later chapters. It is enough to say here that the evidence that all adult symptomatology is "in character" implies that the etiology of psychopathology is in fact no more than a special case of character development in general. Perhaps one should say that it is no *less* than a special case of character development, for this means that such etiology is far more complicated than the conception of any particular and direct cause—any particular developmental conflict, trauma, or other particular cause—might presume.

At the beginning of this chapter I argued that psychopathology is too complex psychologically to have direct and simple neurophysiological causes. But we are bound to assume the existence of some elementary organizing and regulatory system from birth, and therefore bound to assume, also, some innate biological foundation for it. Biological foundations of temperament, of various kinds of sensitivity to the environment, and of cognitive equipment in general must affect the quality of individual experience and individual reaction from earliest infancy. Such foundations must be one determinant, not directly of psychopathology, which involves internal conflict and its ramifications, but of the general form of developing character.

The development of psychopathology—that is, the arrival of internal conflict and anxiety, and of the restrictions and distortions of character that forestall anxiety—will require pathogenic circumstances. But the nature of such development, even to some extent the individual definition of pathogenic circumstances, will be determined also by the existing personality, the existing organization of attitudes, sensitivities, reaction tendencies, and such. In other words, pathological character *development*, like particular symptoms, must also be in character; that development must proceed, so to speak, from the inside, through transformations and differentiations of what already exists. This means that the presence of internal conflict and anxiety will press individual development toward hypertrophy of those anxiety-dispelling propensities, generally inhibitory, already in existence.

The existence and the conservative effect of an organizing and regulatory system argues for a principle of continuity of development, at least a limited continuity. Such a principle of continuity should hold also for the development of psychopathology, rather than a principle, say, of fixation and regression. But this will be a continuity of general regulatory structure, of general ways and attitudes, and in the case of pathology will not preclude relatively abrupt symptomatic changes and changes of affective state.

This general principle of structural continuity should be applicable also to the onset of psychosis, schizophrenia in particular, although that is probably its hardest test. The onset of schizophrenia in the adult, although typically not so abrupt as sometimes imagined, is perhaps the most striking discontinuity to be observed in clinical work, and the processes involved in that calamity are poorly understood. Terms like "decompensation" commonly used in psychiatry to describe the onset of schizophrenia are at best vaguely suggestive and more likely misleading.

Can one say that the onset of schizophrenia, though obviously a real enough discontinuity in many ways, still obscures an underlying continuity of pathological development? I will try to show that this is the case. I do not believe that the distinction between neurotic and psychotic conditions is only a matter of degree. But I will try to show that the exaggeration of the kind of rigidity and passivity that characterize neurotic or nonpsychotic pathology will lead at *some* point in *some* individuals to the emergence of schizophrenic symptoms. In the sense that these symptoms can be seen to retain a formal relation to the preschizophrenic makeup, it might even be said that schizophrenia, too, is "in character."

Clarification of the formal relation of neurotic conditions to schizophrenia must look in two directions: It must examine neurotic conditions for the presence of those formal features that have been thought to distinguish schizophrenia, such as a loss of reality, weakening of ego boundaries, and degradation of affective quality; and it must, also, consider the form of schizophrenic symptoms themselves. A review of the cognitive processes typical of the two conditions, neurotic and psychotic, is particularly important to this study, for these processes are obviously central to their respective relationships with the external world. While the cognitive impairments of schizophrenia always have been apparent, though not always clearly defined, neurotic conditions have generally been considered cognitively intact. In fact, that difference between the neurotic and the psychotic is usually thought to be the most essential one. We shall see that this distinction between the two, though real enough, is not a simple one. The relationship with external reality is not an entirely separate domain, independent of the individual's relationship with himself, for either the psychotic or the neurotic person. We shall see, in fact, that both relationships suffer, in both conditions, from the curtailment of volitional direction.

CHAPTER 2

Dynamics of Self-Regulation

THE THERAPEUTIC PROBLEM OF DYNAMICS

The psychoanalytic conception of dynamics has presented problems not only theoretically, but also therapeutically. It is not hard to see why. The most fundamental aim of dynamic psychotherapy is the enlargement of self-awareness, and in particular the enlargement of the patient's experience of personal agency. This means an increased clarity of his feelings and intentions, of his having wanted and chosen to do what he has done, and of his intention and decision to do what he is actually doing. The patient who initially believes (or tries to believe) that he "can't" stop drinking, despite his efforts to do so, comes to realize that he has reasons to drink, and that he has not, in fact, wanted or intended to stop. To put it differently, psychotherapy aims to make unnecessary, and in this way to dissolve, the self-estrangement that is central to psychopathology. In regard, at least, to the treatment of particular symptoms through the patients' recognition of their unconscious motivations, this aim has always been recognized in psychoanalysis. It is now understood, also, in regard to the patients' direction of his life in general. But it has come to be recognized that the traditional psychoanalytic conception of dynamics is not entirely consistent with that therapeutic aim.

Insofar as early psychoanalysis understood the neurotic individual to be moved, at least in his symptomatic behavior, by unconscious forces or mechanisms, it pictured him as passive, almost as a marionette (Erikson, 1950). The communication of that theoretical conception, intended to enlarge the patient's agency by introducing him to his unconscious motivations, failed to implement its own aim. When the analyst communicates a picture of the patient's passivity before the unconscious forces and mechanisms said to be responsible for his action, he enters, as Schafer (1976) puts it, into a "collusion" with the patient's own disclaimers of intention. Even the correctives of ego psychology, with its greater respect for consciousness, and the present-day therapeutic emphasis on the "here and now" cannot undo the limitations of the conception of adult pathology as an unconscious living out of the family dynamics of childhood.

One can perceive in many therapeutic approaches, both outside of psychoanalysis (Gestalt therapy, reality therapy) and, also, within it, the conscious effort to avoid this problem of the classical theory of dynamics and to enlarge the patient's experience of the intentionality of his symptomatic behavior directly. The most explicit psychoanalytic effort is Roy Schafer's. Schafer proposes that the analyst substitute terms of (often unconsciously) purposeful action, or what he calls an "action language," for the impersonal language of psychological causes and dynamics "in which thoughts and feelings happen" and "mechanisms operate." Schafer's language casts not only behavior and thought, but virtually all motivations and emotions, past and present, as action (". . . we replace the idea of happiness by the idea of doing actions happily" [Schafer, 1976]). His program, in my opinion, both goes too far and not far enough. The attribution of intention is too broad, while its mere assertion, especially when it is so generalized, is not sufficient to solve the problem theoretically or, I would think, therapeutically.

Hellmuth Kaiser, much influenced as an early student of Wilhelm Reich (Reich, in his emphasis on the patient's "way of being," often spoke in "action language"), takes it as axiomatic that the restoration of the patient's experience of agency—his term is "responsibility" (not in a moral sense)—is equivalent to therapeutic cure. He proposes that this can be accomplished by consistent therapeutic attention to the ways in which the patient's speech and immediate behavior fail to express, or avoid, his genuine feelings, wishes, and intentions (Kaiser, 1955/1965). In other words, Kaiser proposes to enlarge the patient's experience of agency by a consistent attention to the most immediate and general ways in which he avoids that experience. One might say that Kaiser, who himself wrote very little, employs action language, but does so precisely where the action is, the immediately present speech and behavior of the patient. I have elaborated a therapeutic method of this kind and its theoretical basis elsewhere (Shapiro, 1989).

Ultimately a solution to the therapeutic as well as the theoretical problems of the traditional psychoanalytic conception of dynamics requires a more inclusive conception of dynamics. The distortion and abridgment of the experience of agency in psychopathology requires in particular a clearer understanding of the subjective processes of volitional action itself, including the conscious processes of intention and decision, and how those processes participate in the dynamics of the psychopathology. That would be a dynamics of the person, of the self-regulative workings of character as a whole, as opposed to a dynamics of particular unconscious forces and mechanisms within the person.

Psychoanalysis has taught us that symptomatic behavior has causes, but they are not causes that move a person passively like a marionette. The causes are attitudes, thoughts, subjective states that, though perhaps unrecognized by him, prompt a person to think and act in ways that forestall or minimize discomfort and, by his lights, are the only ways to think and act.

The Source of Anxiety: Memory or Character?

Freud said, "The adult's ego ... continues to defend itself against dangers which no longer exist" (Freud, 1937/1964, p. 238). The idea of the active, though unconscious, presence in the adult's mind of anachronistic childhood conflicts and anxieties has been central to virtually all dynamic understanding of psychopathology. The conception offers a solution to the most conspicuous problem of psychopathology. The symptoms and anxieties that seem irrational, even to their subject, must have a source. What source could be more plausible than childhood "dangers which no longer exist"?

Yet this understanding has always had its limits: Why a symptom of this particular kind? Why this defense and not that one? Freud himself recognized this insufficiency (Freud, 1913/1958, p. 131) and it has been recognized by psychoanalysts since. With time and an expanded idea of what constituted symptoms, the limits of this understanding have become more evident. To explain the content of an obsessive idea or a compulsive ritual or even a paranoid delusion as an expression of particular childhood anxieties is one thing; but to explain general attitudes and characteristic ways of living, such as impulsiveness or a lack of spontaneity or a rigidly defensive arrogance, is quite another. In other words, an explanation of this kind is unlikely to explain the *general, characteristic, adult form* of symptoms. The particular childhood anxiety is too narrow a base on which to imagine such general aspects of character to have been constructed and to continue to be sustained. Indeed, if early memories and anxieties are, in fact, still vital in the adult, it is much easier to believe that they are so because they have been endowed with significance by, or in some way embody, more general dynamics of the adult character.

Freud's conception of the adult's ego defending itself against "dangers which no longer exist" was founded on a picture of the mind's organization that was still quite rudimentary. In this conception anxiety had a regulatory function, but an extremely simple one. Anxiety functioned as an inhibitory signal, primarily of particular external dangers, such as castration or abandonment. It was triggered in the neurotic adult by the revival of early wishes or fantasies that entailed such dangers. Yet, as I said, one can easily see the theory's logic. An unconsciously preserved childhood idea of some kind of *external danger*, such as a threat of punishment, seems indeed the only way to account for pathological anxiety in the adult *in the absence of a picture of the individual character organization*. Lacking a picture of how anxiety might be generated by the workings of the pathological character itself, as early psychoanalysis did, the assumption of an external danger, or rather, a memory or fantasy of an external danger, can hardly be avoided. But as soon as an individual personality organization is taken into account, an altogether different source of anxiety appears, one that is not dependent on any idea or memory of external threat and, instead, is intrinsic to the regulation and the stability of the personality itself.

Our clinical experience teaches us that kinds of character develop, kinds of attitudes that organize consciousness, that are intolerant of propensities of the individual himself. The rigid and moralistic individual, for example, is discomforted by his own sexual interests. This intolerance, however, will extend not merely to particular wishes or actions; it will extend to whole categories of motivation and reaction and even to kinds of attitudes that are inimical to a given character and are threatening to its stability. Let us say, then, that when these inimical attitudes, motivations, or reactions are, so to speak, activated, when they approach consciousness embodied in specific intentions, they trigger anxiety. Anxiety, in this conception, therefore, is a response to a threat of a different kind from that of external danger, namely an internal structural threat. It is a threat that does not depend on memory, but on the structure of personality.

Actually, Freud's last and most structural conception of one source of anxiety, "superego anxiety," no longer did rely completely on the threat contained in the idea of an external punishment. That threat was at least partially replaced by the internal structural threat of "punishment" by the superego. But the change was incomplete, for an idea of parental prohibition and punishment was still assumed to stand behind the superego.

There is a way to test this proposal that anxiety is not an anticipation of "dangers which no longer exist," but a direct sensation of threat to the existing character. It can be tested by examining the individual quality and content of anxiety in persons of particular character. For anxiety has many different qualities and contents, and if this view is correct, it follows that the particular quality and content of pathological anxiety will depend upon the nature of the individual character and its attitudes.

Consider the following examples:

> A patient in psychotherapy, who is often angrily exercised about old injustices as well as new ones, on this occasion hesitantly, grudgingly, "*admits*" an unexpected satisfaction. At once, she becomes disturbed. She says that (by admitting this satisfaction) she is allowing herself "*to settle*" too easily, "*accepting a compromise*" of "half a life."
>
> An obsessive man, usually scrupulous in observing his rule never to miss any "opportunity," does pass up a chance for an assignment on account of its inconvenience. He tries to reassure himself, first with the thought that the chance will, after all, probably come again, then with the view that, in any case, he really hasn't missed much. But these arguments fail to accomplish their aim, and he becomes more upset. Finally he says that this "might have been [his] real chance" and that it was "*cocky*" to pass it up.
>
> A timid young woman remarks to her therapist with great hesitancy that she notices he has gotten new eyeglasses. She adds that it makes her feel "nervous" to say something "so personal." It seems, she says, "*impudent*," even "*brazen*."

Each of these individuals recoils anxiously from his own action (which may be only an action of thought or speech) and from the threatening sensation of himself that the action evokes. In each case the quality and content of that sensation and the anxiety it evokes is determined by the nature of the individual character:

In the first case, the expression of a personal satisfaction raises the specter, in the mind of this militant individual, of the abandonment of moral protest and a humiliating surrender.

In the second case, a departure from the strictures of duty is translated by a rigid obsessive scrupulousness into a heedless and irresponsible action.

In the third case, an inoffensive, but personal communication is experienced as an audacious presumption by an individual who has learned to keep her place.

Each of these utterances constitutes an act and embodies an attitude that is inimical to the existing character in a specific way, and each evokes anxiety of a specific quality. Rather than saying that an unconscious idea of a particular danger triggers these anxieties, one might say the reverse: Any idea of danger that may be implied by these anxious sensations of surrender, cockiness, and brazenness, as well as their specific qualities, will be the creations of the prohibitions of the individual neurotic character.

The experience of anxiety in these cases does not require the assumption of a conscious or unconscious idea or memory of danger of any kind. It is not dependent on an intervening idea or on a calculation of danger. Although in these cases the specific quality of anxiety was articulated ("brazen," etc.), that conscious articulation was probably a product of the therapeutic situation; it is not typical of the experience of anxiety and certainly is not essential to it. Only the sensation of its threatening quality—vague, fleeting, perhaps not even recognized—is sufficient to trigger the self-regulatory dynamics of character, the self-regulatory processes that we describe as the processes of defense.

Regulatory systems in general do not require ideation; they require only thresholds of sensitivity and processes that set corrective reactions in motion. Anxiety can be compared in this respect to the sensation of pain. Pain might be said to "signal" a threat of further damage to the organism and thus to trigger processes that forestall such damage; but we use the term "signal" metaphorically in this connection, for the process typically does not involve ideational content. We jerk our hand away from a hot pan not because we have an idea or an image of damage to the skin, but because it hurts.

When I say that the occasion and the nature of pathological anxiety will be determined not by the adult's memories but by his character, I imply that the pathogenic conflict has, as it were, been transferred from its original source and content to that character. Let us assume that the child's early experiences of anxiety were in anticipation of some actual or imagined external danger, such as a danger of punishment or abandonment. Suppose that among such experiences some will have been especially intense or continual and will have had a lasting and pathogenic effect. What will be the nature of such an effect? Will it consist mainly of the memory or idea of the particular real or imagined danger, unconsciously preserved and, as Freud believed, separated from the developing personality? Or will its main effect consist precisely of its influence on the developing personality, and therefore be of a more general and characterological kind?

Let us imagine the second alternative, that some pathogenic childhood experience of anxiety, whether on account of real trauma or in expectation of imagined dangers, has the result not only, or perhaps not at all, of memories, but of a change in the child's personality and attitudes. Let us suppose further that such a change in personality will consist, in general terms, of the development of some sort of anxiety-forestalling attitudes. These will presumably be inhibitory attitudes of some kind, perhaps timid or passively obedient attitudes, or rigidly dutiful or careful and guarded attitudes. Such a development will be, in its direction at least, a pathological development.

Once that development of inhibitory or restrictive, anxiety-forestalling attitudes is underway, the child is no longer the same. Before, he was only a frightened child; now, he has become a passively obedient or timid child. Before, he was frightened of a particular real or imagined danger, and he may well continue to feel threatened by what consciously or unconsciously revives that particular danger. But now, as a timid or passively obedient child, he is threatened by much more than that particular danger or any reminders of it. The nature of what is threatening to the child now is no longer determined only by particular memories or fantasies, but by his present attitudes or personality, by what he has become. If he has become timid, an inconsequential initiative will now feel audacious; if he has become carefully obedient, a trivial infraction will seem grave to him.

The infraction, perhaps even the intended infraction, will feel audacious or gravely disobedient not because it revives the memory of a real or imagined punishment, but because it is experienced from the standpoint of a timid or rigidly obedient child, and *because it embodies an attitude inimical to that timid or obedient character.* Indeed, it is likely that the subjective sensation of that threatening attitude itself, an attitude that may be embodied in many different kinds of intention, or perhaps no specific intention at all, will arouse anxiety. And out of that anxious sensation of disobedience or reckless audacity all kinds of threatening consequences can be conjured up.

In a similar way, any pathologically restrictive character will be threatened not merely by particular actions or motivations or circumstances, but by general categories of actions, motivations, or circumstances. Thus a guarded, paranoid person will feel vulnerable and anxious in a wide range of circumstances. Even surroundings that are innocuous, except for being unfamiliar, such as a new restaurant, where he may meet expectations for which he has not practiced and "might look ridiculous," are threatening.

In this way the dynamics of the neurotic conflict loses its dependence on its origins and is transferred to the workings of the personality. The character pathology thus becomes autonomous and self-sustaining. Whatever the particular anxieties responsible for the formation of a pathologically restrictive character may have been, once that character is in existence, the necessity to forestall more general anxieties will work against its relaxation.

There is another aspect of this picture of dynamics that deserves special notice, particularly by psychotherapists. The explanation of pathological anxiety as a signal of dangers that no longer exist depends, for its plausibility, upon the idea of dangers that are objectively great, even horrendous, such as castration or abandonment. Other psychoanalytic theories of anxiety also posit an experience or imagination of great dangers, such as "disintegration" (Kohut, 1971) or "annihilation" (Hurvitch, 1991). In all these, it is assumed that an imagined danger must be great enough to explain the intensity and permanence of the reaction. From the standpoint of a dynamics of character, on the other hand, no such assumption is required. It is no longer necessary to posit an ideational step in the regulatory process or an unconscious calculation of danger. One need only assume thresholds of tolerance *of the individual character* for various propensities or reactions that are inimical to its stability. The more rigid the character, for example, the lower the threshold of anxiety will be for certain sorts of spontaneous action. The reaction of the personality, or rather of the person, to motivations or intentions that are threatening and therefore repugnant or intolerable to him is reflexive and immediate, uncalculated.

This picture, I believe, is much closer to the clinical reality than the traditional one. What we see clinically, in neurotic people, at least, is anxiety—or, more often, an intensification of anxiety-forestalling reactions—evoked by far less dramatic, far more mundane intentions or circumstances than have been assumed. But these are intentions or circumstances of kinds that are intolerable to particular individuals. For one person, to break his rule and pass up an "opportunity," for another, to pay a mild compliment to her therapist, *embody attitudes* that to these individuals feel threatening ("cocky"; "brazen"). The actions involved are of no objective consequence, but the anxiety they evoke is not superficial. The breaking of a rule, for this rigid man, the venturing of that personal compliment, for this timid woman, are not small matters. Nor are they merely ideational transgressions. They will have ideational content—the rigid man may conjure specters of further, appalling transgressions and horrendous consequences—and they may well be associated with particular memories, some more accessible and articulate and some less, but it is the attitude they embody, not the memory they evoke, that is threatening. It threatens the existing character; indeed, in a small way it represents a threatening change of the existing character.

There is admittedly a circularity, or at least an unusual direction, in the logic of this conception of dynamics. It is a circularity that is not present if one regards the pathology as the direct effect of a specific pathogenic agent, such as a traumatic memory or a particular infantile conflict. Why is this rigid person so anxious about passing up an opportunity? Because he is rigid, because he lives according to rules, because *to someone who lives according to rules*, spontaneity, however innocuous, constitutes an abandonment of rules, feels like reckless defiance, like hubris.

This structural conception of the dynamics of character has, therefore, a curious implication for the relationship of anxiety and defense. We are used to thinking that the defense is required by the nature of what must be defended against. But once the pathological character assumes the anxiety-forestalling functions of defense, the process also must be read in the other direction: The nature of the restrictive character determines what evokes anxiety and what must be defended against. To the rigidly controlled individual, a small spontaneity evokes the specter of a loss of control.

THE MEANING OF DEFENSE

The personality's regulatory system must include not only a signal or a trigger for corrective reaction when its stability is threatened, but also the means for such correction. At least as important, it must include a means of forestalling instability. We owe to psychoanalysis the fundamental conception of consciousness-limiting agencies that perform exactly those functions. In psychoanalysis, of course, they are the ego's mechanisms of defense; in the view I am advocating, it is the much more inclusive character itself. I now want to consider the problems of the one picture more closely and to clarify the other.

The problem of a dynamics that casts the person virtually as a marionette is not merely one of language, nor is it inherent in any conception of internal forces and agencies. It may be granted that the description of these internal forces and agencies has often been too literal, anthropomorphic, and voluntaristic. But such description, understood as metaphorical, is commonplace in scientific discourse ("water seeks its own level") and seems harmless enough. The trouble is not only that the language of forces and mechanisms is more than convenient metaphor in psychoanalysis, and is integral to its theory of dynamics. It is, also, that these forces and mechanisms are conceived as operating within and essentially separate from the conscious person, unconsciously and invisibly (Anna Freud, 1937), the results of their operation being reflected in a passive consciousness. It is this gap, at the very least this unclarity concerning the relationship between consciousness and what is unconscious, this apparently innocuous passivity of consciousness in the dynamics of pathology, that contains the therapeutic and theoretical problems. It is this picture of a passive consciousness that departs from clinical reality. For what one sees clinically is the conscious individual very much an active participant in the processes of defense. Not that he can deliberately arrange his own dynamics, of course, but he is quite active in executing them.

For example, the rigid person who is discomforted by any personal choice or decision *actively seeks* rules that can be applied to the situation. The discovery of such rules relieves him of the sense of making a personal choice. Thus he asks himself what the correct thing to do would be, the appropriate thing, the right thing. In the restaurant, he considers what would be the healthy choice or the best value, though he has no great concern with health or economy.

The active and conscious, though unknowing, defensive dispelling of anxiety is even more evident in instances of obsessive indecision, typically instances in which no satisfactory or decisive rule can be found. This indecision has in the past been considered an expression of a deeply rooted ambivalence. Actually, however, the ambivalence is not the cause, but the product of a defense process, though not an entirely successful one. In certain situations where personal choices cannot be avoided, the rigid, obsessive person who feels himself inclining toward a decision experiences an anxious sensation resembling a sensation of recklessness ("I might be making a mistake!"). This anxiety prompts a careful review of arguments against his present leaning. This process, often repeated many times in each direction, often agonizing (although agony is not its aim, only its cost), and often ending in a quick leap of decision, nevertheless has the effect of dispelling the threat of a full and clear consciousness of a personal choice.

The defense processes that I have just cited consist of the active workings of an existing style in particular ways to *dispel* anxiety on particular occasions. But it is the continuous existence of the style, with its essentially stable organization of attitudes and ways of being—for the rigid character, the loyalty to routine, the regular reliance on moralistic rules, proprieties, and such—that constitutes the fundamental anxiety-*forestalling* defense and that regulates stability in a continuous way. All this, also, involves the active working of consciousness.

The psychoanalytic conception of defense is as a drive-energy controlling agency. The mechanisms of defense, in that conception, are understood to operate by denying the unconscious drive-inspired wish or fantasy access to consciousness, thus forestalling conflict and anxiety. Derivative energy-control notions of "impulse-control" and "loss of control" also appear quite widely in psychiatric description. As the reader will see, these concepts present theoretical and therapeutic problems comparable to those of this view of defense itself.

As basic as the conception of drive-energy controlling agencies has been in psychoanalysis, neither the origins nor the precise nature of such controls has ever been clear. David Rapaport, the best known contemporary exponent of the conception, admits, "Little is known about the nature of the process by which (these controls) arise" (Rapaport, 1950). Rapaport often spoke of biological thresholds of drive discharge as possible nuclei of such "countercathexes," and in discussion he sometimes suggested the analogy of a sandbar that accumulates bulk and obstructive capacity from the action of the flow against it. But this analogy does not lead us to any psychological actuality.

The original model of defense was repression. The overall conception of defense as a consciousness-inhibiting agency of some kind, denying consciousness to traumatic memories or threatening wishes, is a generalization of that model. It is in that model of repression that the idea of some kind of counterforce or control, whatever its origins, seems clearest and most plausible. The idea of such a controlling agency seems suited, also, to certain other clinically recognized defense processes, for example, the mechanism of reaction-formation. In that case it is easy to see the possibility, say, of exaggerated attitudes of altruism as a structure of control, particularly of angry or resentful feelings, although a theoretical exclusion of the participation of at least unknowing conscious activity here is questionable. But very often the case is not so simple or straightforward even as these instances seem, at least on first inspection, to be.

There are many defense processes, anxiety-forestalling or anxiety-dispelling processes, including a number of the well-known mechanisms, which are much too complex to be regarded simply as counterforces or impulse-controlling structures, or whose effects are not what one would expect from the action of counterforces. For example, there is no doubt that a defense process is at work in the paranoid individual who insists that an external agent is insinuating female sexual desires into his mind. In that case, however, neither the desires nor the fantasy is inhibited or excluded from consciousness. The effect of the defense process is, rather, the individual's loss of awareness of his relation to, or responsibility for, that desire and fantasy.

The fact is that the basic model of defense as a control structure that denies access to consciousness is not an adequate conception of the self-regulative, or defense, process. As soon as one recognizes the dynamics of character as a self-regulating system, the nature of defense appears in a new light. The defense mechanisms can then be seen simply as features of that system. These processes are not "used" by the person, as is sometimes said; they are processes, constituents, of the person.

Consciousness was originally conceived in psychoanalysis as a passive, registering instrument, after the model of a sense organ. It followed from this general conception, that the processes of defense, as well as the wishes and fantasies defended against, must be located in the unconscious. If intolerable wishes and fantasies were censored, they logically could only be censored *before* reaching a passive consciousness. But today we see consciousness very differently, not as a passive instrument of registration but as actively constructing, integrating, and organizing experience. Furthermore, we recognize that subjective experience is organized in characteristic ways. Individual styles of cognition and thought, as well as the qualities of motivational and of affective experience, are consistent with the organization of the personality and its attitudes as a whole. For instance, the cognition of certain rigid characters is exaggeratedly careful and exact, sometimes too literal and lacking an appreciation of context; impulsive, opportunistic types, on the other hand, avoid the action-inhibiting constraints of reflectiveness and planning, and make judgments on the spur of the moment. Such activities of consciousness easily can be seen now to occupy a central role in the psychological regulating system, including the restrictive, anxiety-forestalling processes of defense.

In sum, the consciousness-restricting functions of defense are performed by the workings of the mind that organize and give shape to consciousness in general. In light of this, it becomes superfluous to posit further controlling or inhibiting mechanisms specifically blocking access to consciousness. The effects that have been attributed to mechanisms blocking or distorting particular thoughts or feelings can be accounted for by various styles of mentation that restrict and distort the general quality of subjective experience. I shall discuss later, for example, the rigid, defensive bias characteristic of the cognition of paranoid people. When that defensive bias becomes extreme, the distortions of reality that are its products are precisely those that are otherwise attributed to the mechanism of projection.

Any organizing process can be said to have an inhibiting or controlling aspect, and any consciousness-organizing mental activity has likewise such an aspect. This can be illustrated in the development of motivational and affective experience in general. The infant's objectification of the world, his increasing awareness of the figures and things of the world, brings with it a consciousness of aims and an increasing intentionality of action.* This intentional or volitional capacity gradually supersedes the infant's earlier global and immediate reactiveness. The general quality of subjective life, the quality of cognitive, motivational, and affective experience, is changed. An aspect of that change can be described as inhibitory in the sense that immediate and diffuse reactiveness is diminished. But the diminished immediacy of reaction is only an effect of the development of more advanced forms of motivation. Any assumption of additional mechanisms of control or restraint is unnecessary.

Something comparable can be said about adult experience and the much confused issue of self-control or "willpower." The existence in adults of diverse and long-range interests and durable emotional ties makes many immediate temptations easily resistible. To be more exact, a subjective context of that kind makes what might otherwise be such temptation less tempting or not tempting at all. This effect is not a product of self-discipline or willpower or any other form, conscious or unconscious, of impulse "control." It merely reflects the fact that the existence of interests and plans creates a perspective from which the immediate circumstance is viewed. One

---

*See Chapter 2 of my *Autonomy and Rigid Character*, Shapiro (1981).

can say that such a perspective constitutes an organizer of consciousness that determines the subjective quality of the immediate circumstance. In this sense, those interests and plans might be said to function as "impulse control mechanisms," although in fact that is not their design.

Forms of consciousness develop along with development in general. It is, of course, very well known that the quality of cognition undergoes development throughout childhood, but forms of motivational and affective experience develop as well. In general, motivational experience becomes increasingly planful and action becomes increasingly deliberate. In other words, volitional action, accompanied by a sense of agency and self-awareness, supersedes earlier forms of passive-immediate or rigid reactiveness. But even in the adult, by no means is all action fully volitional, that is, guided by clear, conscious aims.

Developmental derivatives of earlier modes of action, of both a passive-immediate and a rigid sort, remain within every adult's repertoire. These modes of action, being less fully volitional, entail a diminished self-awareness and, particularly, a diminished sense of agency. We are far less aware of ourselves and our intentions when we react immediately and unthinkingly, or when we inattentively follow routine, than when we make a conscious decision. The repertoire and organization of various modes of activity are highly individual; they are, in fact, a fundamental aspect of individual character. The guarded person allows himself little spontaneity, and then only in very limited circumstances; the impetuous person avoids deliberate, planful action and is comfortable only when large areas of activity are left to the spur of the moment.

In psychopathology, defensive styles have developed that forestall anxiety by limiting and distorting self-awareness and the experience of agency. These defensive styles are characterized by the hypertrophy of developmentally early modes, or derivatives of such modes, of diminished self-awareness and sense of agency. I will show in later chapters that the diverse forms of psychopathology can be understood as instances of hypertrophy of those modes of diminished agency.

A COGNITIVE BASIS OF CHARACTEROLOGICAL DEFENSE: DOGMATISM AND PARANOID KNOWINGNESS

The workings of any characterological defense is a complicated affair, so it is useful to illustrate here, at least in a small way, the general view of characterological defense I have just offered. I shall describe only a particular aspect of such a defense. Both the dogmatic attitude of certain compulsive individuals and the related paranoid attitude of knowingness contain, in different degrees, an anxiety-forestalling illusion of exaggerated capability or mastery of a certain sort, and both are founded on a restrictive and biased style of cognition. Consider the following example of how a cognitive mode can organize and, in doing so, limit subjective experience, and how such cognitive modes are in that way constituents of characterological defense:

> A political activist, who is also quite dogmatic, makes a pronouncement with characteristic assurance: "Reagan will lose the election, believe me." A listener objects, "But the polls show he's way ahead." The scornful response: "Do you actually believe the polls?"

The attitude of superior authority that we recognize in the dogmatic person is a borrowed authority. It reflects the emulation, by one who feels small, of figures or images that, to him, loom large. It reflects a wish and a continuing effort to identify himself with such figures or images that have never been satisfied or successful and have resulted only in a stilted performance for others and for himself. An aspect of that emulation is the substitution of views that in some way carry the stamp of superior authority for a genuine individual judgment. In this way, the experience of independent judgment and the attitude embodied in independent judgment, an anxious experience for one who feels small, is avoided. This anxiety-forestalling process constitutes a defense. But it is not accomplished by any defense mechanism in the sense of an independent unconscious control structure or counterforce. The anxiety is forestalled by the active identification with, or emulation of, superior authority.

The dogmatism that is sometimes an aspect of that emulation, the sense of knowingness, has a cognitive basis also. It is dependent on a specific cognitive style, the rigid and narrowly focused style generally characteristic of compulsive people. This is cognition characterized by a continuous consciousness of purpose. A purposefulness of this kind inevitably entails a bias. It will not allow attention to what does not serve its aims or expectations. What satisfies these aims or expectations is noted; what holds no promise for that satisfaction is brushed aside ("Do you actually believe . . . ?"). The product of this kind of cognition is not only an easy and more or less foregone conclusion but is also a sense of knowingness.

A similar but more extreme form of this attitude of superior knowingness is often observable in paranoid individuals. Sometimes, in these people, it is a suspicious knowingness, sometimes a defensively arrogant knowingness, sometimes both.

> For example, a paranoid man enters a therapist's office for the first time, glances quickly around, and says, with a disdainful air: "No doubt you're recording this. I don't mind." (No recording equipment was present, and no recording was being made.)

The attitude is familiar to psychological testers: Another rather paranoid person, about to take the Rorschach inkblot test, sees the cards, glances quickly at their backs, smiles stiffly and with a faint contempt at the tester, says, "Oh, yes, the Rorschach, of course, I've had it before, a bat," and flips the card on the table. His condescending smile, together with his comments "of course" and "I've had it before" seem intended to convey, "I know what you're up to. It's not even worth dodging."

> A more severely paranoid man expresses a similar attitude more frankly; he says of his fellow patients in a sanitarium: "They don't want to have anything to do with me. I know too much."

The purposefulness of paranoid cognition is more intense and its selective bias consequently more extreme than that of the merely dogmatic person. The confirmation of paranoid expectations is accordingly much easier and quicker, and the illusion of knowingness consequently greater, sometimes even grandiose. In both the dogmatic and paranoid cases, therefore, the defensive illusion of cognitive mastery rests on actual cognitive sensation.

SELF-DECEPTION

Defense processes operate both to forestall anxiety and to dispel it. Although these are by no means absolutely distinct, it is the dispelling of anxiety, or the effort to dispel it, that is particularly instructive. I have suggested that the processes of defense, the processes through which self-awareness is distorted or restricted in the interest of forestalling or dispelling anxiety, do their work in the course of the organizing of conscious experience itself. These dynamics often culminate in the phenomenon that I have characterized elsewhere as "self-deceptive speech" (Shapiro, 1989). In speech of that kind, one sees the actual processes of the distortion of self-awareness microscopically, but often vividly.

> Here is an example: A freelance worker, having no definite commitment for a job he hoped to get, has just made the difficult decision to accept a less satisfactory one. He tries to dispel his misgivings about the decision unsuccessfully in this instance. He says, emphatically, "I'm *sure* I did the right thing! . . . (more quietly) I think."

It is important to remember in this connection that speech is not just language. Speech is action that employs language. To borrow from the English philosopher of language, J. L. Austin, saying something is doing something (Austin, 1962). Normally the aims of speech-action are communicative—promising, warning, sharing a joke or information, and so forth. But the speech-action that we are considering is different. It is not so much aimed at communicating with another person as affecting the speaker himself. It is talking, in other words, primarily for the speaker's own ear, in order to dispel or revise some disquieting thought or feeling, typically a thought or feeling of which the speaker is not clearly aware, yet one that is close enough to awareness to be threatening. Hence, self-deceptive utterances often take the form of emphatic assertions of conviction, as in the example above ("I'm *sure* I did the right thing!"). Frequently, repetitions ("I'm *sure* I did the right thing! I'm *sure* I did!") serve the same aim. Speech of this kind is an effort, unrecognized by the speaker, to convince himself of something that he does not believe or to feel something that he does not feel. It is not a reflection of a defense process that has already been accomplished. It is an active continuation, often a culmination, of such a process.

Actually it is not only in efforts to dispel anxiety that self-deceptive speech is recognizable. It is present more continuously and in many characteristic forms in the forestalling of anxiety. The clinical significance of this kind of speech was indicated first by Hellmuth Kaiser in an exceedingly interesting observation. Patients, Kaiser said, don't talk straight (Fierman, 1965). Kaiser explained that although they might be perfectly sincere, neurotic people seemed without exception to give the impression of some artificiality or ungenuineness in their speech; what they said did not seem to express what they actually thought or felt. The tears sometimes seemed forced or worked up; the story of childhood sounded rehearsed; the angry account of yesterday's event, as one listened to it, had the quality of a public oration. It was artificial, but there was no suggestion of a conscious intention to deceive the listener. In short, what Kaiser observed was self-deceptive speech.

The importance of Kaiser's observation is not only in his identification of self-deception of this kind as a regular even central symptom of all psychopathology. Apart from that, the observation makes it clear that self-deception is not a completely internal process. That is to say, the process itself, not only its results, can at least in part be directly observed in speech. Nor is this defense process entirely unconscious. Although self-deceptive speech obviously is not consciously and deliberately planned—that is, its *aim* is not conscious—it clearly involves some degree of conscious activity and effort.

That active effort is consistently observable, if one looks carefully enough. Statements of feeling, for example, often do not reflect what is revealed in the speaker's expression. Sometimes feelings are denied in their report, but sometimes they are exaggerated. The patient in psychotherapy describes his unhappiness, but the description and his gestures seem melodramatic and forced. Or, he speaks of being furious, but does not look furious. He says dramatically, "I hate my father!" but it turns out that he thinks he "should" hate his father, although he actually feels sorry for him. In these cases, also, the self-deceptive utterance itself constitutes an active defensive effort.

It seems, in fact, in such cases, that the self-deception and indeed the whole process of defense receives its final construction in speech. It is possible that all self-deception is finally constructed in speech, either to oneself or to a listener; certainly it seems true for a large class. It would not be remarkable if this were so. We recognize now, after all, that a genuine feeling or belief achieves its fully conscious form in speech; the same might be expected of a self-deceptive effort.

SELF-DECEPTION AND
THE RELATIONSHIP WITH EXTERNAL REALITY

There is another characteristic of self-deceptive speech that is noticeable to the listener that confirms its essentially noncommunicative nature and reveals another aspect of the process of defense. When a speaker says, "I'm *sure* I did the right thing!" or some such thing, with exaggerated emphasis, one does not have a sense of being addressed or even seen in the ordinary way. The speaker's voice is often louder than a normal conversational voice. He does not seem to be looking clearly at the one he is addressing. One does not seem to be in his focus; his look seems to be distant. The listener easily might feel tempted to wave his hand to catch the speaker's attention. That attention seems inward, in the way of someone listening to himself, much like a person who is practicing a speech.

It is true that in some instances this inwardness of self-deceptive speech takes another form that at first does not seem inward at all. Sometimes the speaker looks directly and searchingly at the listener's eyes. The response he sees, or thinks he sees, in the listener's eyes has a special importance to him; he is remarkably sensitive to it. A confirming response from the listener produces visible relief, while the slightest hesitation is quite discomforting and often prompts the speaker to renewed efforts. Despite his apparent concentration on the listener, however, the speaker, here, too, is actually addressing and listening to himself. His concentration on the listener's expression is misleading; he is watching the listener in the way one looks carefully in the mirror for signs of a blemish, losing awareness of the mirror itself. He is addressing himself through the listener. This is sometimes further confirmed when one happens to interrupt the speaker abruptly and he reacts with an embarrassed laugh, as if noticing the listener for the first time and, it seems, noticing himself, as well.

It appears, in other words, that at least in the more urgent, anxiety-dispelling forms of self-deceptive speech, the speaker has lost the normal objective awareness of both himself and his listener. The sense of separation from the listener, the "polarity" of speaker and listener, to borrow the developmental psychologist Heinz Werner's term (Werner, 1948), is markedly diminished. The processes of defense, on that occasion and in this respect, at least, have weakened the normal relationship with, and the normal interest in, external reality.

The loss of a clear sense of what one believes or feels or wants to do, as a result of defensive restrictions or self-deceptions, is at the same time a loss of a clear sense of what one believes or feels or wants to do *about something or someone*. The relationship with oneself and with the external world are in that way inseparable. The defense process is not a matter of internal dynamics alone. A weakening and a distortion of the experience of external reality inevitably accompanies a loss or distortion of self-awareness. The neurotic person who feels small and insignificant overestimates the importance and worth of the other one. The obsessive person, unsure of what he wants, "realizes" after he has made a choice that what he rejected was far more desirable.

The processes involved in this last type of distortion are not hard to discover. The anxiety of making a personal choice ("Maybe I should have . . . !"; "Maybe I really wanted to . . . !") drives the obsessive person to review the alternatives, even after the decision has been made. But that anxiety determines, also, that the review will be distorted. The missed chance will be recalled with a rueful and unforgiving bias. Only those elements whose loss might be regretted will be recalled, and a picture will be constructed of someone or something now painfully desired. That distorted image of an external reality is not a product of the ordinary process of judgment, of looking things over. It is a product, rather, of a kind of moral discomfort, the anxious concern that a choice should not be made, if at all, without careful review for any possibility of a mistake; and a possible mistake should not pass without remorse and unpunished. In this way, it reflects the complication, perhaps even the displacement, of the ordinary relationship of the individual to external reality by the internal dynamics of self-deception. Typically, regular judgment returns and the rejected "opportunity" loses its shine if it becomes available once again.

The distortion of self-awareness and simultaneous distortion of external reality can work in the opposite direction as well and sometimes can be confirmed in an interesting way. The abandonment of a self-deception with a recovery of the individual's genuine feelings, as may happen, for instance, in psychotherapy, invariably has the additional result of a clearer picture of the object of those feelings. The man who has long insisted that he really wants to end his relationship with a certain woman begins, perhaps, to realize that in fact he does not want to do that, but only thinks that he should. As he becomes aware of his actual feelings, he presents to both the listener and to himself, for the first time, a clear picture of the person who is the object of those feelings. It is no longer a picture drawn to persuade himself to leave her, but his actual picture of her and one therefore that is consistent with his behavior. Thus a clearer experience both of the self and of the external figure emerges from a vague and tendentious construction of that figure. One might say that the "polarity" between the self and the external object of interest has at that point been reestablished.

Louis Sass, in his discussion of schizophrenia, has suggested that delusional ideas are not so much believed as they are reflections of a suspension of disbelief (Sass, 1992). I think he is right, but the notion has a more general significance and a wider application than that. It applies to all self-deception. That is to say, the products of self-deception are not genuinely believed in the ordinary sense. That is why self-deceptive speech is so artificial, exaggerated, and repetitious. That is why, also, a genuine but discomforting belief that has been avoided or denied may suddenly intrude ("I'm *sure* I did the right thing . . . I think"). And that is why self-deceptive statements are not reliable predictors of action. People by no means actually do all that they say and think they want to do, or, for that matter, discontinue all that they say and think they do not want to do. It is, actually, not only a suspension of disbelief that is involved in self-deception, but a suspension of disbelief *or* belief. It is, in other words, a suspension to some degree of the normal objective interest in external reality, in compliance with the requirements of internal dynamics. In short, some such suspension of the normal relationship with external reality is an aspect of the processes of defense. As such, of course, it is by no means always fixed and stable, and never without tension and effort.

SITUATIONAL SELF-DECEPTION

The kind of self-deception we have considered so far is driven by individual conflict and anxiety. Its content is determined by the nature of that anxiety. But there is also a kind of self-deception that is driven by external threat or coercion: The confessions produced by Chinese "thought reform" or Soviet-style show trials; the "recovery" of doubtful traumatic memories at therapeutic insistence; the "remembering," under duress, of criminal acts never committed; the admission, by the bullied wife, of deficiencies that are none too clear to her. These are not cases simply of submission—the decision to give them what they want—or of persuasion to new beliefs; they are, again, the products of another form of thinking, another frame of mind, altogether. They are worth studying not only for their intrinsic interest but, also, for the further light they throw on pathological dynamics and, specifically, the processes of defense.

In all these cases the normal attitude of judgment is suspended or disabled, in some cases even consciously so, at least within the relevant area. Sometimes a suspension of critical judgment or "rational thinking" is explicitly required. For example, in a widely publicized case of alleged sexual abuse of children, one of the accused, under intense pressure to remember and confess, was instructed to "not try to think about anything" (Wright, 1994).* Probably more often the normal attitude of judgment is simply disabled by inhibition in the face of coercion.

---

*I am told that methods of induction of hypnotic trance also commonly include the request to avoid critical thoughts.

In any case, it seems that the various forms of coercive "thought control" or "brainwashing" do not operate in a simple or direct manner, but rather through a mediating process in which the normal interest in reality is lost. Existing convictions, it appears, cannot be directly expunged from the mind and new ones inserted by coercion. But the disabling or inhibition of active judgment can be accomplished. To put it more sharply, what one knows one knows, and there is no way not to know. But knowing the answers is not enough if there are ways to prohibit asking oneself the questions.

The evidence is strong that the person subjected to coercion never does come to believe that he did what he did not do. But he can be brought to the point where he is unable to sustain disbelief. More exactly, just as internally driven dynamics can force an abandonment of ordinary judgment in favor of an alternative construction of reality, coercion can force a similar abandonment of the normal interest in reality and the ordinary attitude of belief or disbelief. The bullied and intimidated wife does not dare even to look at her angry husband. Much less can she consider clearly what he is saying and, perhaps more to the point, what he is doing. From her standpoint, merely to consider him, to look at him or evaluate what he is saying, is an act of brazen defiance. In these circumstances, only passive acceptance and "agreement" can dispel anxiety. It therefore happens that the coerced subject joins the coercive effort. The intimidated wife finally reminds herself of her supposed failings, perhaps even of failings that are not entirely clear to her.

In much the same way, the accused sex offender in the case just cited finally agreed that he remembered the acts he had initially denied. It was noted by a detective present at the time, however, that the language of his confession was filled with "would've's" and "must have's." At the conclusion of his confession, the accused man said, "Boy, it's almost like I'm making it up, but I'm not." Another of the accused, in the same case, also recovered "memories" of acts she had initially been unable to remember. She, too, remarked that this memory was "different" from her "normal memory."

The experience of these people seems to be identical to that reported by Robert J. Lifton (1963) of subjects of Chinese "thought reform":

> One such person says: "You begin to believe all this, but it is a special kind of belief."

Lifton speaks in this connection of a "surrender of personal autonomy." He notes the peculiar manner of speech of those still influenced by their "reform" experience: as "speaking only in cliches," "parroting . . . stock phrases" (p. 117), and such. It is clearly not a conversational manner of speech, speech aimed at communication of genuine feeling or belief to the listener. It is ritualistic speech. What Lifton observes is the evidence of an anxiety-dispelling reaction to the coercive situation.

It seems, in fact, that the defense reactions triggered by anxiety whose source is external are the same as the defense reactions triggered by internally generated anxiety. We can identify in these cases of coercion the same psychological processes that we observe in psychiatrically familiar, character pathology. Thus the anxiety-forestalling passive, uncritical state of mind that is familiar in more or less stabilized form in hysterical character appears to be identical with the state of mind found in cases of "recovered memory." It includes, in either context, a readiness to defer to authoritative opinion, to accept ideas and eventually to "believe" them, or rather to think that one believes them. One could characterize each of these conditions, also, as a "surrender of autonomy."

Other defense processes familiar from psychopathology are also discernible in some coerced confessions. The efforts by rigid, compulsive people not only to do but, also, to think and even feel what they "should," and the self-deception in which they dutifully imagine that they do think and feel what they should, are known to us. This condition is yet another form of "surrender of autonomy." It might be compared to that of a soldier whose independent judgment is suspended in favor of a literal adherence to regulations. Accordingly, these people sometimes arrive at conclusions that can be comprehended logically, but are unrealistic to the point of absurdity; their speech is full of far-fetched "must be's," "could be's," and "might be's" (the tiny spot on the pizza, since it is red, "could be" blood; it "might" have come from an infected handler . . .). Ideas such as these, as their "might be's" and "could be's" reveal, are not genuine judgments of reality. They are not genuinely believed, but they cannot be dismissed without great anxiety.

The processes I have just described, with their partial or temporary abandonment of genuine judgment of reality, operate also to produce the confessions that are a common outcome of Soviet-style political show trials. I do not mean that those processes are merely analogous to those that operate in coercive circumstances, but that they are identical. The anxiety or terror of the situation can be dispelled only by the suspension of interest in reality and the acceptance of, even conscientious participation in, the accuser's rules of "logic," a logic also typically full of "must have's."

Thus, Artur London, who describes the conditions ("You must trust the party. Let it guide you.") that led to his confession of political crimes in Czechoslovakia, says: "It was no longer a matter of facts or truth, but merely of formulations, a world of scholastics and religious heresies" (London, 1971, p. 173).

London's wife, who eventually accepted her husband's guilt, says: "It was not possible for me to be right and the party wrong" (p. 304). In other words, she did not dare do other than suspend her own judgment and, in doing so, the normal relationship with external reality. Her statement is an explicit expression of the dynamics of self-deception, driven in this case, presumably, by a combination of internally generated anxiety and externally induced terror.

I cannot close this discussion of self-deception without referring to the philosophical problem that has surrounded it, particularly since the problem may adhere, as well, to the general concept of internal defense. Self-deception can easily seem paradoxical. As it has been put by philosophers: How can one intentionally, knowingly, not know? The process clearly requires a selective monitoring of oneself, and that selectiveness has been taken to imply both knowing what must not be known and at the same time being able not to know it. If the problem has not troubled psychoanalysts, their solution has not satisfied philosophers. Psychoanalysts can posit an independent unconscious agency, the ego, that can intentionally deceive the conscious person. In this way the problem of separating the deceiver from the deceived is accomplished, but only by reifying a descriptive concept, creating a "smart" unconscious, and in the process creating just that picture of a passive consciousness that is problematic.

The paradox disappears from the standpoint of the dynamics of character, without the assumption of a planful or "smart" unconscious. Certainly self-deception implies a self-monitoring process of some sort and it implies a self-regulating process as well. But the assumption that the monitoring process or regulatory action has to be smart or knowing or absolutely separated from consciousness is altogether unnecessary. All sorts of regulatory action works reflexively and unknowingly. As I pointed out earlier, we jerk our hand away from the hot plate not to protect the skin, but because it hurts. Self-deception does not require knowing what we must not know; it requires only a regulatory system that can be triggered by inimical ideas or feelings while they are still incipient and that can react in ways that forestall further conscious development of them. Individual character constitutes just such a regulatory system. It combines both the monitoring and the restrictive functions.

THE LARGER SYSTEM OF DEFENSE

When one foregoes the concept of defense mechanisms in favor of the more comprehensive picture of self-regulation, it is easy to see that defense, the forestalling or dispelling of pathological anxiety, involves not only strictly internal processes but, also, various sorts of overt action and often external arrangements as well. The culmination of defense processes in self-deceptive speech is an outstanding example of such action, but there are many others. I shall discuss some of these systems of defense in detail later, but it is useful to illustrate the point briefly here.

Consider the case of hypomanic individuals, with their artificially expansive spirits and exaggerated self-confidence. This defensive adjustment, often none too stable, is aimed at forestalling painful self-criticism and depression. But its success appears to require not only continual self-congratulations and self-flattery ("Last night I was gorgeous!") but, also, a forced "spontaneity" and constant, speedy, perhaps even in some way successful, action. This kind of activity and driven spontaneity are not merely products of elation, as is commonly thought; they are essential constituents of elation and they are critical to the defensive aim of avoiding self-critical judgment. Maintaining this activity, furthermore, requires external arrangements: The extravagant ambitions must have objectives; the often urgent desire to entertain requires an audience of some kind. The continuous, even driven, purposefulness of compulsive people is a similar example. That purposefulness obviously needs external objectives. These are usually found in the form of work, especially of a kind whose accomplishment can be clearly measured.

I want to emphasize that this activity and these arrangements are not merely products of the dynamics of defense, but components of those dynamics, essential conditions of the personality's self-regulation. The defense system, in other words, like the self-regulatory system of any living organism, is an open system.

It is well known that in nonpsychotic pathology, at least, the defense organization and the attitudes it involves also have adaptive aspects. The compulsive's productiveness, not infrequently even the hypomanic's productiveness, the hysteric's social appeal, in some circumstances the psychopath's capacity for quick action and, up to a point, the suspicious person's eye for the hidden irregularity all may have adaptive value. These adaptive capacities reflect the essential nature of the defense processes. In other words, the adaptive advantages of defense styles are not cumulative results of adjunct capabilities attached to the defense itself; they are capabilities intrinsic to those styles, and their adaptive value may well have been important in their development. The adaptiveness of a defensive hypertrophy of certain tendencies demonstrates again, in fact, that defense is not simply an inhibition or control of feeling and motivation, but a revision of their form that may have been fostered not only by the need to forestall anxiety but, also, by the opportunities offered by the circumstances of its development.

SECTION TWO
PSYCHOPATHOLOGY, AGENCY, AND VOLITION

CHAPTER 3

Abridgments of Volition

Motivation is usually treated objectively in psychological theory. It is usually treated as a force, a drive, or an impetus of some sort. Even when motivation is treated somewhat more subjectively as wish, it is seldom with reference to its individual subjective form. Much the same can be said of the treatment of action; its individual quality—impetuous, deliberate, hesitant, or such—is rarely considered. Most often, psychological theory simply assumes that when motivational impetus reaches a certain intensity, action results. Actually, one can hardly consider the individual form of motivation and action without considering the psychology of volition, and both psychoanalysis and psychology in general have preferred to avoid the matter of volition, with its burden of old philosophical problems. But in doing so they have neglected the significance, particularly for psychopathology, of the various kinds of abridgment and curtailment of volitional processes and the distortions and compromises of volitional experience.

In the human adult, almost no action of consequence is a simple, immediate reaction of need to object. Action is never totally without anticipation, imagination, and consciousness of itself, except perhaps in the case of the most severe pathology. Needs, wishes, affects, opportune circumstances do not directly trigger action; they generate interest in the possibilities of action and, ultimately, they may generate intentions. The intention, not the need or affect, is the most proximate impetus to action.

Unlike the conception of need or drive toward object, intention is the impetus of a person who, according to his attitudes and ways of thinking, is conscious in some measure of the possibilities and effects of action. This is why the quality of action will be as characteristic of the person, in a given situation, as it will reflect the intensity of a need or wish. And this is why the characteristic quality of action and its subjective experience will vary considerably from one individual to the next, more deliberate or less, more spontaneous or more constrained by propriety, more wholehearted or more often on "automatic pilot."

Volitional or self-directed action, action directed according to conscious aims, is a developmental achievment. It is, also, an evolutionary achievment; the capacity for consciously self-directed action is surely essential to the adaptive capacity of humans. But that advanced mental capacity entails, also, certain psychological vulnerabilities. For the capacity for volitional direction brings with it the sensation of active intention, the consciousness of choices and decisions, and the experience of agency and personal responsibility. And these, in turn, may bring a new kind of internal conflict and the possibility of pathological anxiety.

No one fails to achieve the capability of volitional direction, and therefore no one is immune from its costs: its prohibitions, conflicts, and anxiety, to one degree or another. Where conflict and anxiety threaten seriously in the course of development, personality will be pressed to develop in ways that forestall it. I have proposed that such conflict- and anxiety-forestalling development takes the form of a reliance on, and hypertrophy of, prevolitional modes of diminished agency-experience, or more exactly, adult adaptations of such modes. Those passive-reactive or rigid prevolitional modes, in their hypertrophied forms, are manifest in the familiar psychiatric syndromes. What follows will consider more closely their origin and also their adult status.

PASSIVE-REACTIVE AND RIGID MODES

The infant is passive in a special, more profound sense than merely being inactive or submissive. The infant is passive in the sense of being moved in his activity by vital needs or reflexes; he is reflexively or instinctively reactive to what presents itself. It is true that we have learned that this early activity and reactiveness is more complex than was once thought, but it remains essentially a passive activity and reactiveness in this passive sense. The infant is not yet in possession of what Heinz Werner (1948) calls "personal [conscious] motives."

The emergence of such personal motives and of action with a goal in mind and the further emergence of increasingly articulated, complex, and distant goals is probably too gradual to be marked with any precision. Though rapid at the beginning, it is a more extended process than one might think. One can remind oneself of its general quality if one compares not even the infant but the young child's unselfconscious and irresponsible spontaneity of action, his distractibility and the immediacy of his reactiveness with the adolescent's serious, if not always constant, planning for life and highly conscious interest in self-determination. It is a development that may be summarized as one of increasing, and increasingly conscious, self-direction.

At the beginning, the development of active intentionality is closely tied to the child's increasingly objective awareness of an external world. The emergence of conscious aims and of intentional action in pursuit of those aims follows inevitably from the recognition of interesting external objects. The recognition of the rattle creates an interest in the rattle as an object to be grasped. A new object, a rattle, and a new subject, an active rattle grasper, have been created at the same stroke. The beginnings of objectification of the external world are at the same time the beginnings of a new, more active, and more autonomous form of motivation or directedness, directedness according to conscious aims. The development marks not so much a different attitude toward the world as the coming into being of an *attitude toward the world*. Hence Werner's description of a new directedness of this sort as the emergence of personal motivation out of a reflexive or instinctive global reactiveness.

With each advance in the objectification of the external world—recognizing an interesting object, remembering and imagining what is not in view at the moment, understanding something of cause and effect, and so forth—goals are increasingly articulated, and the polarity of self and external world becomes sharper. At the same time, the child's relationship with the external world becomes more active, reflective, and self-determined. The clearer his conscious aims and the wider and more imaginative their scope, the more deliberate and planful his self-direction. Gradually, in a development that continues throughout childhood, the immediacy of the young child's reactiveness is superseded by more deliberate choices and decisions. He becomes a more active agent; it does not seem too much to assume that he also feels like a more active agent.

I have not yet referred to an interesting and, particularly for our purposes, important feature of the child's prevolitional life, childhood rigidity. That rigidity is well known, of course. The child's insistence that things be done "right," that is, exactly as they have been done before, often without regard to altered circumstances or even the logic of achieving the desired goal effectively, is familiar to everyone. Heinz Werner tells us that this rigidity reflects the child's still-global and relatively indistinct grasp of the objective situation, his inability to distinguish what is essential from what is not, hence his "all or nothing" attitude.

It is not difficult to see the passivity of this allegiance to exact routine and habit, and its relation to the kind of passive-reactiveness that I have described. The child's interest, in a given situation, triggers a global memory of, or perhaps a "feeling" for the way this thing is done. His relation to that memory or feeling is a passive one; that route is the only route. One might put the distinction between passive-reactiveness and rigidity this way: Passive reactiveness refers to the child's immediate and quasi-reflexive response to an external provocation; rigidity refers to the passive enactment of a fixed internal program, in this case a memory. Thus, with an increasingly clear and objective picture of the external world, the child's early rigidity, also, is gradually replaced by a more reasoned awareness of his essential aims and a more actively searching and discriminating judgment and self-direction.

There is another critical dimension of the development of self-direction that must be considered at this point, the relationship with the adult world. The child's developing autonomy and sense of agency are, of course, not products only of his own physical and mental development and his own increasing consciousness of an interesting objective world. Self-direction and agency are influenced, also, by adult figures, judgments, and constraints. From the first signs of the child's capacity for self-direction and volitional control, adults have both the opportunity and the wish to exercise a more durable and extensive influence on the child's behavior than was possible in infancy.

Adults are emulated, and the authority both of their behavior and of their judgment determines what is right and wrong, what should be done and how it must be done. Initially, according to Piaget, the authority of adult constraints is accepted concretely as absolute law: Wrong is what is prohibited and punishable by adults (Piaget, 1932). Later, however, adult authority is translated and internalized as rules, interpreted and applied by the child, though still retaining their subjective quality as imperatives deriving from and supported by superior authority. The child's volitional self-direction advances in this way, but to the extent that it is still limited to the execution of authoritative rules, it is still rigid. One might say that the rigidity of established routine is to some extent replaced by the rigidity of adult-derived rules. The child's agency has grown somewhat, but it is dependent upon a borrowed authority.

If development goes reasonably well, as the child becomes an adult, the subjective gap that separates him from the adult world closes. Some rules take root in his own personality, affect his attitudes, and are in turn transformed by them; others are sloughed off. Those rules that have taken root and been transformed in this way lose their aura of superior authority to which obedience, sometimes even literal obedience, is demanded. Such "rules" therefore lose their rigidity; they are no longer rules, but become personal convictions, applicable according to personal judgment. At the same time, this newly adult individual has become aware of a wider world and of new and more distant possibilities, and this awareness, in turn, has changed him into a more planful and deliberate individual. Altogether, he has been transformed from one who is merely reactive to his environment to one who, according to his interests and values, makes choices and actively pursues his aims.

All this is involved in the process that normally leads, self-consciously at first, in adolescence, to the discovery of one's own voice. It is a condition of respect for one's own judgment, of knowing what one wants to do and intends to do. It is an experience of agency and it is founded on the actuality of a genuinely volitional self-direction.

But no one is, in a continuous way, fully conscious of his intentions, or even of having intentions at all. Nor is anyone limited to a single mode of activity. The most planful and deliberate person is spontaneously reactive, distracted, or provoked at times. Much is left to habit and established routine by everyone. Such action is done semiautomatically, with hardly any sense of agency. In such connections, people speak, for instance, of being on automatic pilot.

Authoritative, even rigid, rules of many kinds are convenient for living. They make reflection unnecessary and save energy. They are not followed out of deep conviction, but out of vague acceptance, often not quite acceptance of their usefulness, but of their authority; it is inconvenient to consider them thoughtfully. One drives the way one has been taught to drive, and one's table manners are what they are supposed to be. Many rules—perhaps religious rules, various customs and traditions—we follow simply because it feels wrong or, again, would require inconvenient reflection to do otherwise. In these cases, also, we accept authority, but by no means necessarily because we agree with or understand its reasons or, sometimes, even know their source. In all of this activity, one hardly feels aware of choice or decision, and this indeed is its benefit.

In the development of agency, or volitional self-direction, therefore, earlier, prevolitional modes of action—immediate and spontaneous action, rule- or habit-based action, essentially rigid or passive reactive modes of diminished agency—never completely disappear. Adult, often adaptive, derivatives of these modes develop, and they remain in everyone's repertoire. Far from disappearing, in fact, derivatives of these prevolitional modes may well account for the larger part of our activity. But they have become subordinate to more planful, volitional direction. In matters of consequence, in new or complex situations, at critical points of direction, spontaneous or habitual modes of action are normally suspended. They are superseded, then, by deliberate, consciously directed action.

One drives on the turnpike for long stretches listening to music, talking, daydreaming—driving automatically, with a fraction of full attention. During those stretches, awareness of agency, awareness of the act of driving itself, is much diminished. But when the exit announces itself, or there are signs of an accident ahead, one stops talking and concentrates, and then one feels like a driver again.

A hierarchy of self-direction has developed in which various kinds of spontaneous reactiveness and habitual or rule-directed action, requiring little or no reflection and often less than full attention, and accompanied by a diminished sense of agency, are permitted. This assignment of direction to more or less automatic reactiveness has limits determined for each individual both by circumstances and by character. When circumstances change and those limits are approached, the mode of action changes and the experience of self-direction changes with it. An inattentive interest is displaced by a more careful directedness, or a concentrated and purposeful attitude relaxes. But the assessment of circumstances is a subjective and an individual matter.

The hierarchical system of self-direction is responsible for the variability of each individual's behavior and for the fact that no individual can be completely characterized by a single style of behavior. This does not mean that there is no relatively stable character, or that we cannot characterize an individual in a general way. It only means that "character" is a more complex and elastic system than can be completely described by a single mode or attitude. That system includes not only general tendencies but also the limits and fluctuations of attitude and mode and, with them, of agency-experience in various circumstances.

An interesting example of the hierarchical organization of self-direction is offered by the frequently rather muddled and misleading conception of loss of control. One commonly hears references in psychiatry to "poor impulse control," or the equivalent, in regard to violent or otherwise objectionable behavior, particularly when the subject himself disclaims intention. There is no doubt that such instances often seem initially, and often sincerely feel to their subject, like genuine failures of self-control. Yet, therapeutic work is likely to reveal that it is not the ability, but the wholehearted desire for self-control that is lacking.

It seems that there is something to be said for either view, that the supposed failure of self-control is what it is presented as being, and at the same time that it is not. This ambiguity actually follows from the fact that the system of self-direction or "control" is not simple and unitary, but hierarchical. It is the existence of just such a hierarchy of self-direction that makes it possible for some individuals, much more than others, to *permit themselves*, or even to arrange, a "loss of control" without fully realizing that they are doing so. The executive who avoids close supervision of an impetuous subordinate can more easily disclaim responsibility, even to himself, for that subordinate's behavior. He can thus permit actions or results that, if they felt deliberate, would be impermissible. This is an example of the defensive possibilities of the hierarchical direction of action.

When the direction of activity is left mainly to its own momentum or to routine, self-awareness and the sense of agency are generally faint and peripheral. But the experience of agency—the clear consciousness of doing what one wants to do, of having chosen to do what one has done—is, also, quite acute at times. When one consciously departs from the routine or no established routine exists; when one disappoints expectations or there are no expectations to respect; or when a careless, spur-of-the-moment reaction is impossible (even for those to whom it might come easily) because the action is protracted and reflection and self-consciousness are therefore unavoidable—all these are times when self-awareness and the experience of agency are likely to be keen.

We know, on the evidence of psychopathology, that just such self-awareness and experience of agency is for some people acutely discomforting, not only in connection with particular motivations but more generally in connection with living. Such experience, then, is reflexively avoided or at least diluted by a reliance on, even a general limitation to, prevolitional modes of activity, passive reactive, or rigid modes of intrinsically diminished agency. Attitudes and ways of thinking have developed—I will describe such attitudes in some detail shortly—that embrace those modes and have become general and characteristic. The organization of such attitudes and ways in individual character becomes the principal means of forestalling anxiety, the system of defense. As yet we know little of the external conditions or predispositions responsible for such developments, but we can make some very general surmises.

If we are right, the normal attitudes and modes of diminished agency of childhood will become the source materials, so to speak, of the adult system of defense. Particular passive-reactive or rigid modes, already available, will be relied on not only to forestall anxiety as required but also as they are favored by external circumstances. Such modes may hypertrophy, and may also become limiting. Let us say, for example, that the anxiously obedient child becomes, in particular circumstances, a pleasant, but unusually docile, even timid adolescent. Normal initiatives, perhaps even serious ambitions, will seem audacious, generate anxiety, and be inhibited. In short, a self-regulating system, a neurotic character, will have come into being, with its own dynamics and its own tense stability.

In the following two chapters, we shall consider some specific, diagnostically familiar, nonpsychotic conditions in which the prevolitional modes of passive-reactiveness and rigidity are manifest: passive-reactive modes and attitudes as they are represented in hysterical and impulsive-psychopathic conditions; rigidity as it appears in obsessive-compulsive and paranoid conditions. Each of these conditions is usually regarded as a discrete psychiatric syndrome (and at least one case, the obsessive-compulsive, is even considered by some to be a specific neurophysiological disease). We shall see in some detail that for each pair the apparently disparate symptoms and different, though less disparate, attitudes that those symptoms embody are actually derivatives of quite closely related modes. In fact, it is possible to define with some degree of precision the relation, in each pair of conditions, between the two representatives of the general prevolitional mode in question.

While the modes that are represented in these conditions are derivatives of developmentally early ones, I want to emphasize once again that this does not imply a regression. It does not imply, either, that the adult pathologies in which these modes are represented can be ordered according to a linear developmental scale. The fact that various forms of passively reactive and rigid modes are employed by all adults makes an assumption of regression unnecessary. One needs only to assume that these modes, already available, may hypertrophy in the course of development.

The further assumption that these hypertrophied prevolitional modes may undergo various adaptive modifications during development and may have various pathological and adaptive ramifications allows us a far more realistic picture of adult psychopathology than a regression hypothesis offers. For the stubborn fact remains that adult pathology cannot really be fitted into childhood prototypes. The young child, say, does not really resemble the adult psychopath, even if the psychopath's impulsive, opportunistic mode of action has historical sources in the child's immediate reactiveness to what is before him. That reactiveness achieves that pathological adult form only when it has been integrated with cynical, opportunistic attitudes that can only be acquired later. It is entirely possible, in fact, that those later conditions that foster cynicism turn the developing character decisively toward a defensive reliance on that prevolitional mode. Altogether, rather than regression to stages of early development, we must look toward the adaptation or defensive employment of what has been retained from early development.

CHAPTER 4

Passive Reactiveness

The conditions to be considered here vary greatly in symptomatic behavior: the emotionally labile hysteric, mildly impetuous, often vague of purpose, easily influenced; the opportunistic psychopath, sometimes calculating, sometimes reckless, emotionally neutral; the "weak" individuals, who feel unable to resist either temptation or external pressure. These kinds of character and their symptoms seem so diverse that one might easily doubt the justification for gathering them into a single category.

Yet, to see their fundamental likeness of character it is only necessary to notice what is conspicuously lacking in, even avoided by, all of them. It is the experience and the actuality of planful and considered action. It is in this sense that these individuals may all be described as passive. It is not that they are necessarily passive in the behavioral sense of being slow to act or docile or tractable. They are passive in the deeper sense of lacking to one degree or another in reflective, conscious direction of their own behavior and lives.

To put it otherwise, all these people are characterized by a diminished sense of personal agency, or responsibility for their own action in that particular way. This is not a moral charge, but a psychological fact: Their action often does not feel to them altogether intentional or deliberate; frequently it feels taken against their will. They feel, and they say, in one way or another, "I can't help myself"; "I didn't know how to refuse"; "She pushed my buttons"; "I lost it." The psychopath says, "It was just sitting there, so I took it"; the hysteric says, "I'm ruled by my emotions." It is true that such statements are sometimes exculpatory pleas, exaggerations of diminished agency in protest of innocence. But such exaggerations are not likely, probably not even possible in a convincing form, unless the actual experience of agency is diminished. The psychopath's disclaimers of responsibility (*How did you get in trouble again?* "Everytime I get out, somebody puts a gun in my hand"; *Why did you beat him?* "He resisted") are only defensive exaggerations of an actually diminished experience of responsibility.

I want to consider particularly two varieties of this general passive-reactive mode: the hysterical character and the opportunistic, psychopathic character. I have chosen them, first, because, as psychiatric categories go, they are fairly well defined and easy to picture. They also are strikingly dissimilar symptomatically and for that reason can be used to demonstrate certain points clearly.

I want to show several things: First, that these two kinds of character represent two adult adaptations of anxiety-forestalling prevolitional modes. Second, that the respective forms of their principal symptoms are expressions of these modes. Third, that they are adaptations of passive-reactive modes of different degrees of reactive immediacy (perhaps originally of different levels of maturity) and therefore of different degrees of diminished agency. Finally, that a general relation of the two conditions of passive-reactiveness can be defined in these ways, and that such a general relation is confirmed by a consistent correspondence of their respective symptoms. Thus, these are not the discrete diseases that psychiatric custom assumes. Nor can their respective symptoms reasonably be considered derivatives of early conflicts or traumas, particular to each, and stored in memory.

TWO KINDS OF "SPONTANEITY"

I am of course stretching the common usage of "spontaneity" here. We can easily describe the emotionality and lively reactiveness of the hysteric as spontaneity, but it may seem strange to apply that term to the opportunistic or reckless action of the psychopath. Yet these are in fact two kinds of spontaneity, two kinds or levels of comparatively immediate reactiveness. The dissimilarity of their symptoms has accustomed us to see them as altogether unrelated, although George E. Vaillant notes that, when immobilized, the psychopath is hardly distinguishable from the so-called primitive hysteric (Vaillant, 1975).* Their characteristic attitudes, the cynicism of the one and

---

*A relationship has also been noted in the empirical-psychological literature. See C. R. Cloninger (1978).

the romanticism of the other, do indeed at first seem quite remote from, even opposed to, each other. However, as I will try to show, these differences are not inconsistent with the sort of relation between them I have suggested; they only help to define it.

It is worth recalling here something of the early relation of emotion to action. In the infant's earliest reactiveness there is hardly a separation between the two. Emotional experience is intimately connected with somatic-motor activity (Werner, 1948). As action becomes progressively more intentional, however, it separates from emotion. Emotions, feelings, continue to be immediately reactive to the external event, but with development they no longer are sufficient to trigger action. Feelings become motivational factors, incentives to action, but action itself becomes increasingly reflective, instrumental, and planful. In other words, action becomes the product not only of immediate feelings but, also, of more distant interests.

From the time the infant's global reactiveness differentiates in this way into an immediate consciousness of feeling, on the one hand, and the beginnings of volitional action, on the other, genuine loss of control of action becomes increasingly doubtful. For the adult, immediate emotional reaction may tempt action, but can no longer trigger it. The separation of affective reaction from volitional action is accompanied, also, by the increasing differentiation of affect itself into more specific emotions.

I mention this development particularly in order to clarify a puzzling aspect of the relation of the two kinds of spontaneity we are considering. One thinks of the impulsive psychopath, who is often moved even to reckless action, as being in that way more reactive, or at least more primitive in his reactiveness, than the hysteric. Yet it seems that he reacts with less, not more, emotion. Indeed, the psychopath is often described as "cool" or affectively neutral. The early relation of affect to action makes this apparent paradox understandable.

We may speak of the sort of emotional experience characteristic of the hysteric as labile or even shallow, but it is a developmental achievement, nevertheless. It is a reactiveness in which emotion is, on the whole, clearly separated from action. The reactiveness of the impulsive psychopath, by comparison, is a less differentiated reactiveness. Psychopathic action, although often calculating, is by no means indifferent. Temptation or provocation are more immediately and urgently translated into action and, particularly in the case of provocation, frequently accompanied by abrupt flashes of anger. The two conditions represent adaptations of different, though closely related, prevolitional modes, one developmentally some-what more advanced in its origins than the other.

Psychopathic Character

Impulsive and opportunistic psychopathic individuals fall, perhaps most plainly, within that category traditionally called "character disorders" in psychiatry. Psychopaths have been considered, among psychiatric conditions, distinctively free of anxiety and of subjectively unwelcome or "ego-alien" symptoms. In other words, psychopathic, or sociopathic, character has traditionally been regarded as a more or less consistent distortion of the whole character. This is considered to contrast with neurotic conditions whose symptoms, including anxiety, are regarded as products of continuing internal conflict. In recent psychoanalytic literature there has in fact been considerable theoretical discussion of the more general question of whether certain psychiatric conditions, of which the psychopathic character would be an example, are pathologies of developmental arrest and deficit, rather than of internal conflict.

The idea of developmental arrest seems quite doubtful. It overstates the resemblance of adult pathology to childhood and seems to ignore the considerable variability of function observable in all people, not excluding even schizophrenics.* The possibility of various kinds of psychological deficit, on the other hand, is quite real. It may well be an aspect of much or all psychopathology—not, however, to the exclusion of conflict, more likely a factor in determining its form.

The distinction, in general, between disorders of character, on the one hand, and neurosis, on the other, is in my opinion no longer supportable. The evidence is strong, as I said earlier, that the symptoms of all psychopathology, certainly all nonpsychotic conditions, are consistent with the general styles of the character in which they appear, and psychopathic character can no longer be considered distinctive in this respect.

Nor is the relative absence of anxiety as distinctive to the psychopath as might be imagined. For the most part, what we see clinically, not only in psychopathic character but in psychopathology in general, is not so much anxiety as the variety of ways in which anxiety is avoided. It is true that in some forms of psychopathology, including the psychopath's, anxiety is

---

*For a similar criticism of the idea of developmental arrest, see Morris Eagle (1987).

avoided more successfully than in others, but this hardly argues for a fundamental difference between it and other neurotic conditions. It only underscores the effectiveness of the psychopathic mode of quick, unreflective action in diminishing self-consciousness and the sense of agency, and thereby forestalling anxiety.

It is not the case, either, that the absence of anxiety in psychopathic individuals is absolutely consistent. Numerous clinical observers describe uneasiness, defensiveness, paranoid and depressive reactions, "and other affects usually viewed as absent in the psychopath" (Person, 1986), particularly in conditions of restricted action. Indeed, it has been noted by Person and others (for example, Vaillant, 1975) that the impulsive and erratic action that is generally characteristic of these people, the frequent changing of jobs, relationships, and locale, seems precisely what is for them necessary to dispel anxiety. The psychopath, in other words, forestalls anxiety by "acting out." Hence his need always to be in action. In short, the impulsive action of the psychopath is a defense.

There is another kind of evidence, also, that supports that view. It is common for psychopathic and impulsive individuals to rely heavily on alchohol and drugs. These substances further diminish self-consciousness and the experience of intention or agency. They seem important adjuncts to the anxiety-forestalling mode of immediacy or "spontaneity" of action.

> Thus a middle-aged man with a long history of exposing himself briefly to young girls admits, indeed emphasizes, that he is a "weak" person, a person lacking in self-control. He says (in his defense) that he does this only when drinking. However, he expresses no wish or intention to stop drinking.

Many traits of psychopathic or impulsive character that might otherwise be considered simply as deficiencies of character actually require reinforcement, and therefore appear in defensively exaggerated forms. Thus the individual just cited not only prefers to think of himself as "weak," rather than as the intentional author of his action; he also actively tries to "weaken" himself further. In other cases, psychopathic recklessness is supported by an artificial bravado, opportunism is reinforced by a defensive cynicism.

All this implies not merely an existing defect or developmental deficiency of agency, reflectiveness, or conscience, as some would argue, but an active avoidance of those experiences. To put the matter more comprehensively, this picture suggests that if there are such deficiencies, such as a deficiency of reflectiveness, they are employed and exaggerated in the interest of forestalling anxiety. Perhaps something of the sort can be said of all psychopathology: Any developmental deficiencies of character that may exist are likely to be employed defensively.

There is, finally, yet another kind of evidence that argues against distinguishing psychopathic character from other kinds of pathology that show more obvious signs of internal conflict. This evidence is admittedly theoretical. It is the relation of psychopathic character to other forms of defensive passive-reactiveness, in particular the relation to hysterical character that we are considering here. The very correspondence that I will try to show of the traits of the one condition to those of the other, reflecting a consistent relation between the two kinds of pathology, seems to me the most persuasive argument of all that these are two varieties of neurotic character that are distinguished mainly by their reliance on passive-reactive modes of somewhat different quality.

The trait, or deficiency, that is most commonly thought to be basic to the opportunistic, psychopathic character is a deficiency of conscience or superego. There is no doubt that this deficiency is real, but it is quite doubtful that it is basic. The common conception attributes a whole character structure to what is only a particular expression of that character. There cannot be an effective conscience where there is only a faint experience of agency. No amount of moral instruction can take root where the experience of intention, and therefore of personal responsibility, is faint.

Not only a weakness of conscience, but many other psychopathic traits that are often attributed simply to that weakness, actually follow directly from a diminished sense of agency. For example, the well-known tendency of these individuals to externalize responsibility ("As soon as I get out, somebody shoves a gun in my hands") reflects not only a denial of culpability by a person of weak conscience, but, more fundamentally, the defensive exaggeration of an actually diminished experience of intention.

There is a particular corollary of the quick reactiveness of the psychopath that is important to the understanding of a number of psychopathic symptoms. A reactiveness of this kind is consistent only with an egocentric view of the world. A reactiveness that quick and unreflective can only produce a subjective world limited to the here and now, to that which strikes the most immediate interest or concern.

The most obvious reflection of this subjective world is the general psychopathic trait of opportunism. This opportunism, also, is usually taken simply as the willingness of a person of weak conscience and few principles to be guided instead by expediency. But, more likely, opportunism reflects the psychopathic deficiency, not of conscience only, but of actively planful self-direction. In other words, it reflects, more fundamentally than a weakness of conscience, the limitations of an immediate reactiveness to what presents itself and the absence of a longer and broader view. For it is that broader view that normally reduces the here and now to a feature in a larger context. Given the absence of such a view, one might even say that opportunism represents a more or less successful adaptation of a passively reactive mode to the adult world.

The psychopathic habit of lying is similarly regarded as a direct reflection of a lack of conscience, but actually involves this more fundamental aspect of character. A lack of conscience would certainly account for a willingness to lie. Whether it would itself account for the fluency of psychopathic lying is less likely. This fluent lying, or general glibness, bespeaks a different relationship with external reality than the normal relationship. Anyone can lie, of course, and under certain circumstances it is entirely possible to lie with good conscience. But the normal person has an interest in objective reality and an awareness of it that, quite apart from conscience, constitute a permanent obstacle to fluent lying and glibness. That relationship with external reality is weakened in the psychopathic person. His interest is limited to more immediate personal matters, to getting by, leaving the desired impression, or avoiding one that is not desired, and he is not inhibited by a stubborn consciousness of the facts of the matter.

Sometimes this limitation of interest to the immediate present is disguised, although thinly. The adolescent delinquent who has dropped out of school says, when he is asked about his plans, that "maybe" he will be a doctor. He is not insincere; but he does not at that moment realize that this implies returning to school. Sometimes, however, the vagueness about the future and the absence of plan or active direction is undisguised. A woman, convicted of stealing checks, puts the matter straightforwardly: "When you're cashing checks, you don't think about getting caught" (Reid, et al., 1986).

It is not necessarily that these individuals live easily in the here and now. They actively avoid contemplation of the future. In other words, this trait is, once again, not only a reflection of a simple deficiency. A deficiency may be there, but if it is, it is defensively employed and exaggerated. One cannot seriously contemplate the future without becoming conscious of one's self and aware of one's intentions, and this is the awareness that the psychopath or impulsive character avoids.

In general, this avoidance is achieved simply by quick, unreflective action. There are other, supplementary, devices, however, whose aim is clear. Sometimes, for example, by restricting attention to the immediate step in what is obviously a further interest, it is possible to avoid more than a dim awareness of that interest, or perhaps to avoid consciousness of it altogether.

For example, an alcoholic patient is about to leave the hospital. He mentions that he is going to a party where there will be a good deal of drinking. He is asked by the doctor whether he intends to drink:

PATIENT: "There's no sense making promises. I've done that plenty of times and then, when the time comes, I break them."

The doctor explains that he had not meant to extract a promise, only to ask what the patient's intentions were.

PATIENT: "No, I can't say, I don't want to make a commitment I can't keep. *I'll see how I feel when I get there.*"

By turning away any thought of his future action, he is able, so to speak, to delegate the decision to the spur of the moment.

The more or less successful avoidance of all but the here and now is very likely fundamental, also, to the fearlessness, or recklessness, or simple heedlessness that sometimes characterizes psychopathic individuals. The image, so familiar in the romantic literature of adventure, of the somewhat psychopathic but fearless rogue who easily risks his life and fortune is probably not entirely unrealistic. The willingness of some criminals, addicts, and alchoholics to risk even ruinous consequences for short-term interests is sometimes understood in dynamic psychology as an expression of unconscious self-destructive aims. But that assumption, implying as it does a clarity of unconscious planning, is unnecessary. It is more likely that planning of the sort that would include a clear consciousness of future risks is simply avoided. One might say that the psychopath's heedlessness of risks is the complement of his opportunism; together, these traits reflect the limitations, and sometimes the effectiveness, of immersion in the here and now.

It is not always easy to separate a simple deficiency, perhaps a cognitive deficiency, from an anxiety-forestalling characterological defense. What may originally have been an agency-diminishing deficiency, such as a cognitive deficiency, may then take on the expanded function of an anxiety-forestalling avoidance of agency, as in a defensive avoidance of reflective planning. Nor is it always possible to assign developmental, or logical, priority to one or another aspect of character. For instance, a paucity of distant and stable aims and interests, whether a result of individual deficiencies or, more likely, hopeless and demoralizing conditions of life, is bound to foster an opportunistic reactiveness to the here and now. For without the normal context of distant and stable interests that temper and qualify immediate opportunities and provocations, those opportunities and provocations will become more powerful. But that opportunistic, spur-of-the-moment mode of action may then become characteristic, defensively functional, and infused with cynical attitudes. At that point, reflective planning and serious commitments will be threatening to its stability and anxiety-arousing. What once may have been out of reach must now be avoided. Ambiguities and circularities such as these are intrinsic to the development and dynamics of character.

HYSTERICAL CHARACTER

To avoid a mode of planful and deliberate purpose, with its sensation of agency and, for some, anxiety, is to embrace a mode of passive reactiveness. The comparative picture of the two varieties of such reactiveness in the two kinds of character we are considering can be drawn simply: The psychopath acts quickly, perhaps recklessly, without self-consciousness or inhibition; sometimes he acts coolly, sometimes out of abrupt changes of mood or interest. The hysterical individual, on the other hand, flushes with emotion; sometimes she acts impetuously, but on a limited scale, mainly in ways of small consequence that give no offense. ("Hysterical character" is often described diagnostically as "histrionic character," but histrionics are not an essential feature of this character. The histrionic manner of some hysterical individuals is merely a more conscious exaggeration of their labile emotional reactiveness. It is a further effort, in other words, to reinforce the characteristic defensive mode and its self-image.)

Thus, psychopathic and hysterical character represent two passive-reactive modes in which, to different degrees, planful, reflective, deliberate action is avoided, and an anxious experience of agency is, in the one case, largely forestalled and, in the other, at least significantly diminished. While a consistent relation can be shown between the basic formal dimensions of the two kinds of character, such as general quality of affect, immediacy of action, and experience of agency, the two conditions diverge and become more individual in their ramifications and symptomatic particulars (Table 1).

Certain attitudes and a particular kind of self-image give the passive-reactive mode of hysterical character its specific and familiar shape. These are the attitudes and the self-image of one who has little sense of personal authority, and who therefore does not dare to claim authority, of a person who does not take herself seriously and does not expect, indeed does not wish, to be taken seriously. It is a character form that is predominantly female, for societal reasons that are familiar (Lakoff, 1977).

> A woman of thirty says that she "cannot" express a political opinion to her father: "It would feel fresh."

Sometimes these individuals are timid, sometimes they are lively and engaging, perhaps frivolous or somewhat irresponsible in an exaggeratedly childlike, harmless way. Their language is often hesitant and vague, full of "ish" suffixes, and sometimes rather childlike. When annoyed, such a person is "grumpy"; when nervous, she is "discombobulated." They describe themselves as ruled by their emotions, and offer their judgments as no more than notions, based not on logic, but on intuition. In doing so, they actively disclaim serious reflectiveness and, in some measure, defensively, disclaim intention and personal responsibility.

Still, the diminishing of agency or personal responsibility that these attitudes and disclaimers express is quite limited as compared to the psychopath's. The hysteric's romantic and defensively exaggerated idea that she is ruled by her emotions, not by thought, clearly reflects a diluted experience of self-directed and intentional action. But, as compared to the psychopath's frank externalization of responsibility, in which a sense of personal participation is virtually absent (*Why did you beat him?* "He resisted"), the hysteric's sense of agency, though diluted, is not absent.

67

TABLE 1 Passive Reactive Modes

	Impulsive-Psychopathic	Hysterical
Mode of Activity	Erratic, reckless, opportunistic, easily triggered action, quick decisions	Mildly impetuous, spontaneous
Sense of Agency	Externalization of responsibility (to circumstance, provocation, opportunity)	"Ruled" by emotions, suggestible
Affect	Abrupt mood changes, some sentimentality, more often bland or emotionally "neutral," egocentric	Sentimental, labile, "shallow" affect, egocentric
Judgment	Short range and egocentric; avoids long-term planning and consideration of consequences	Avoids serious reflection, subjective, vague, "intuitive"
Personal Relations	Egocentric, exploitative, cynical, uninhibited, can be engaging	Egocentric, romantic, highly subjective, engaging, spontaneous
Fabulation	Glib, opportunistic lying	Romanticizes and exaggerates

This difference in the loss, or avoidance, of agency is reflected in the corresponding difference between the general quality or level of the hysteric's impetuousness, on the one hand, and the reckless action of the psychopath on the other. Hysterics are impetuous, but as a rule only in matters of small consequence, like the person of whom it is said that she says everything that comes into her head. Hysterical individuals are on the whole not capable of spur-of-the-moment action that is seriously consequential. Serious action, action of consequence, or the sort of heedless action that comes easily to the psychopath is anxious for the hysteric. This is so precisely because the hysteric is unable to avoid, to the extent that the psychopath can, an *awareness* that it *is* action of consequence, and is therefore unable to avoid the sensation of responsibility that that awareness entails.

Sometimes, it is true, ordinary hysterical flightiness does extend to action whose possibilities of serious consequences seem not to have been noticed. When these consequences arrive a reaction to them of astonishment may reveal clearly the absence of reflection and the diminished consciousness of agency that the action involved.

> Thus a young woman who, after a marriage of only a few months, has abruptly left her husband for a romantic affair with his friend is shocked when he takes action to annul their marriage. She exclaims, "But I was only kidding!"

Even so, this woman's reaction, in its disclaimer of responsibility, is short of the psychopath's view, in comparable circumstances, that he has run into simple, unpredictable bad luck.

The defensive reliance, in hysterical character, on the specific mode and attitudes of harmless, childlike flightiness comes at a subjective cost. The inhibition of deliberate and serious purpose is at the same time an inhibition of an attitude of competence and sometimes even an inhibition of competence itself. These people are mindful of their lack, or imagined lack, of qualifications, particularly in the presence of someone they respect. They overestimate the significance and authority of others; they are suggestible and, in a personal way, easily brainwashed. Most generally, perhaps, they feel like children, or perhaps incomplete grown-ups ("I haven't jelled") in a world of real grownups.

In some of its symptomatic ramifications, the hysterical mode of passive-reactiveness seems far removed from that of the impulsive psychopathic character. To remind oneself of their proximity, one needs only to consider again that it is precisely because the defensive attenuation of agency is less extreme in the hysterical case that anxiety, inhibition, and disclaimers of personal competency are more in evidence.

The correspondence of hysterical and psychopathic traits, at their respective levels of passive-reactiveness, can be easily extended. The relation shows itself, for example, in the quality of affect characteristic of each. The film director Federico Fellini is reported to have said that sentimentality is only a step away from cynicism, and it is not hard to understand his meaning. Sentimentality, often descriptive of hysterical affect (it is not rare, either, in the psychopath), is emotion that is easily evoked and labile, that is furthermore not highly specific to its object and therefore easily transferable. Hysterical affect is often described also, with much the same meaning, as capricious or "shallow." These are the qualities that one might say are "a step away" from the cool insincerity and cynicism of the psychopath, although obviously it is still an important step.

This kind of emotional reactiveness is also characterized as egocentric. It tends to be dominated by immediate personal interests and circumstances as opposed to more distant or abstract and therefore more stable concerns, the kind of interest that Piaget speaks of as "affective decentration" (Piaget, 1981). This, too, might be considered "a step away" from the more frankly egocentric interests of the psychopath that are even more responsive to the changing colors and opportunities of the moment.

There is another familiar aspect of the hysteric's emotional egocentricity. These people endow others, as well as things and situations, with affective qualities that they do not possess. The boss is described as larger than life; the teacher is an ogre ("I hate him!"); even the Rorschach inkblot figure of a bat is "big! scary!" These figures are not seen objectively, in their independent qualities; they are, so to speak, ready-made creations of the subject's feelings. The inkblot bat looks "big" because the one who sees it feels small. This subjectivity is often apparent, also, in the hysteric's extravagantly and sometimes undiscriminating romantic feelings. In this affective sense, perhaps one could say that the object of such feeling is "used" by the hysterical person. If that were so, such use would correspond on a somewhat more advanced affective level to the psychopath's egocentric exploitation of the other one.

The subjectivity of the hysteric is not an affective matter alone. It also concerns her relationship with external reality and with objective truth in general, just as the egocentricity of the psychopath does. The psychopath is known not just for his capacity to lie—we all have that capacity—but for the fluency and ease of his lying. Psychopaths are glib; their stories are easily adapted to the requirements of the situation. This characteristic is, as I said earlier, not merely a reflection of a deficiency of conscience, but of a more fundamental limitation of interest. The psychopath's interest in the immediate demands and opportunities of his circumstances eclipses his consciousness of the objective reality.

Something comparable can be said of the hysterical character. The inkblot bat looks "big" not only because the one who sees it feels small, but also for an additional reason. Normally the inescapable consciousness of the figure's objective existence as an inkblot limits such subjectivity. In the hysteric, that objectivity is not sufficiently present. In this case, too, the immediate subjective reaction displaces consciousness of the objective reality. And, in fact, hysterical individuals are well known for their romantic exaggerations, stretching of the truth, even fabrications, not for opportunistic gain, but less consciously and out of emotional requirements.

It is not necessary to develop the point further. A correspondence of symptoms or traits, persuasive as it may be in more general characteristics, cannot be expected in every detail. Because the two conditions are adult characterological adaptations of closely related, though not identical, passive-reactive modes, each has acquired distinctive adaptive features. Robin T. Lakoff (1977) has pointed out, for example, that the usual picture of hysterical character is virtually identical to a particular socially constructed image of femininity. Such a person clearly may be a social success, even a professional success. Similarly, the psychopath, or, at least, the individual with marked psychopathic characteristics, may in some circumstances be a well-regarded man of action, admired exactly because of his quick, frequently effective decisions and apparent willingness to take risks.

CHAPTER 5

Rigidity

RIGID "WILL"

Is rigidity an excess of will or a disability of will? Is it helplessness or refusal? Anyone's initial impression of rigidity in the form, say, of dogmatism or stubbornness or paranoid resistance is of an overdeveloped will. All these traits seem to reflect an active and deliberate self-directedness that stands at the opposite pole from impulsiveness or other kinds of passive-reactiveness. The rigidity of young children gives much the same impression. Their insistence on doing things the same way, the "right" way, is what we call "willfulness."

Yet, another look at rigidity seems to show exactly the opposite picture. For example, in Goldstein and Scheerer's (1941) classic study of brain-injured adults, they describe the extreme rigidity of their subjects as a helpless "will-lessness," an inability to shift at will from one viewpoint to another, a "stimulus-bound," passively reactive, concrete attitude. Thus the one view sees rigidity as a refusal, while the other sees it as an inability. From the one standpoint, it is an extreme failure of self-direction and a case of utter helplessness; from the other, it is exactly the opposite, an exaggerated exercise of personal will.

The same paradox was noted by Kurt Lewin in his classic study of retarded children. He observed that "the will of the feeble-minded often appears stronger . . . than that of the normal child" and remarked on their obstinacy and "pedantry . . . shoes must stand before the bed in exactly one way . . . " (Lewin, 1935, pp. 204–205). Indeed, Lewin remarks that the adherence of these children to the rules in play gives their behavior an "appealing appearance of moral rectilinearity" (p. 217).

The paradox is no less evident in the various traits of rigid character, and in that connection its subjective aspect is particularly interesting. The dogmatism or stubbornness of the compulsive individual, for example, not only seems to the observer like an excessive exercise of will, but is typically experienced with a sense of pride as strength of will by the stubborn person himself. But when one hears, about that same stubborn or dogmatic person, that he cannot tolerate the slightest variation in his routines, or when he himself unhappily compares his routine existence to the operation of a train on a fixed schedule and a fixed track, what had seemed masterful and strong now seems only helplessly obedient.

The question can also be translated into the terms we have been using: The rigid, compulsive person seems to possess, if anything, an excess of personal responsibility, a sense of agency that goes beyond the normal. His actions, far from being the products of unreflective impulse, are marked by a heavy deliberateness. He holds himself responsible even for what is beyond his or anyone's control, not just for what he does but also for his feelings, for what he is. It seems more than a full measure of agency. Yet he tells us that he has never done what he really wants to do, or that he does not really know what he wants to do. And, in fact, we see that when this same individual is confronted with a personal choice or decision, even one of little objective consequence, he is thrown into a state of anxiety.

The problem can be clarified by a closer look at the psychology of rigidity. According to Heinz Werner (1948), the young child's rigidity, as it appears in his insistence that things be done exactly as before, follows from the child's incomplete objectification of the world. It is the limitations of the child's understanding—his global view of the situation, the fact that its essential elements are not yet clearly distinguished from the inessential, his limited sense of instrumental subgoals—that require the procedure to be done exactly as before. The child has no clear and objective sense of the relation between action and aim, hence an aspect of the situation brings to mind the recollection of the whole procedure, the "right way" to proceed. An interest in the goal triggers an internal program, and the action is reeled off in the habitual way.

One may describe the child's application of rules learned from the adult world in much the same way. Like the global memory of previous experience, such rules determine the right way to do things. This is the mode of action that prompts Lewin's comparison of the retarded child's adherence to rules of play to a strict "moral rectilinearity." We are accustomed to regarding the young child's unquestioning acceptance of adult authority as a natural expression of the child's dependence and the adult's prestige in the child's eyes, but it must reflect, as well, the child's lack of a clear understanding of the essential elements of a situation.

The child's self-direction according to adult-inspired rules is, in other words, not founded on a clear sense of objective realities and does not consist of an active assessment of the requirements of those realities. The adult-inspired rule is, for the time being, an aid to the child's intentional action. Insofar as the child must rely on this aid, his self-direction is still passive. It consists of a "reeling off" of activity triggered by his interest and directed according to a fixed internal program, and to that extent reflecting his still-inadequate grasp of the realities of the situation. It seems reasonable to presume that this process involves less than a full experience of personal choice or agency, but it does involve a clear definition of the "right" way to do things. The child's stubborn "will" is now the spokesman of adult authority, as before its authority was conferred by the memory of earlier experience.

At least as far as the child is concerned, therefore, we can define the meaning of the rigid will with some clarity and resolve the paradoxes that surround it. The child's rigid will is simply his confident idea, in the absence of an understanding of the logical route to accomplishing his aim, that his aim can be accomplished only by the fixed internal program of memory or rules. Hence, genuine self-direction and agency are limited, while at the same time conviction is strong. We will see that something comparable can be said of the rigid adult, although of course the dynamic situation is quite different.

RIGID CHARACTER

Normally the subjective gap that the child feels between himself and the adult world gradually closes. The objectification of external reality develops and with it, genuinely volitional self-direction. We know, however, that development does not always proceed in this way. We see, in rigid character, adults who continue to live under the sway of authoritative rules.

These people, like individuals of hysterical character, have continued to feel less than full-fledged adults and have continued to emulate—without realizing that they do so—remembered or, more likely, constructed images of adults of unquestioned authority and to refer constantly to authoritative rules. For these individuals, the consciousness of such authoritative standards and rules has become so weighty that the experience of personal choice and independent decision has in itself become an audacious and anxious experience. The application of rules and the emulation of authoritative images override and obscure such personal choice ("I *don't know* what I want!"). To some extent, as we will see, the reliance on such rules even displaces the evaluation of external reality. As with the child, genuine personal agency and self-direction are limited, while the exercise of "will," as the representative of the right way, the correct solution, the appropriate thing, is uninhibited.

The psychological function of such rules and models for the rigid adult is, of course, not what it was for the child. They are no longer necessary, as they were for the child, to supplement a cognitively limited capacity for self-direction. Nor is their function the economical one that customs and rules normally serve for the adult. The rules and models that hold sway in the rigid character are redundant. They are relied on by an adult who has the cognitive capacity to direct himself yet does not dare to do so. The authority of those rules and models that was useful and reassuring to the incapable child now inhibits self-direction for the capable adult.

This redundancy of direction has a number of symptomatic ramifications. Perhaps the most general one, present in all the varieties of rigid character, is a special kind of self-consciousness. Self-conscious roles develop that are versions and derivatives of those respected models and rules, adapted to adult circumstances. The lawyer is careful to behave as he thinks a lawyer is supposed to behave. The external manifestation of this kind of self-awareness and self-direction is an unusual deliberateness or stiltedness of behavior. Ordinary action, in which attention is largely focused on its objective, is encumbered by a supervisory attention directed to the process itself.

But an internal supervision of this sort is not always as benign as a mere encumbrance. A rift or tension is created between the individual's spontaneous reactions and judgments and the requirements and directives of his rules and models. These requirements and directives, typically taking the subjective form of a self-conscious, nagging, or urging sense of "I should" or "I must," frequently obscure spontaneous reactions, wishes, and judgments. These people often think that they want to do what, actually, they only feel they should do, or they are at a loss to know what they want to do, or they experience what they want to do in some attenuated form:

A woman who continues a relationship that she insists she wants to end speaks exasperatedly of her attachment as an inexplicable "addiction."

Another person who had long maintained that she "really want(s)" to move to another city, but actually only thought she should, contemptuously attributes her failure to do so to "inertia."

These individuals, in other words, are alienated, to one degree or another, from feelings and motivations that do not conform to their rules and models, their "should's". Such people are often engaged in an effort of (a rule-based) *will* to subdue their own genuine wishes. In these struggles of will, the rigid person's effort to identify himself and what he wants to do with what he thinks he should be and should want to do may be powerful enough not only to demean his actual wishes, but even to make them unrecognizable:

A dignified, elderly professional man says about his occasional bouts of heavy drinking, "I don't *want* to drink! Obviously, something infantile *in me* wants to drink, but *I* don't want to!"

In these cases, the individual's actual feelings and motivations are not only expressed in his eventual action but undoubtedly make themselves felt in conscious, if unrecognized, sensation, as well. Hence the struggle of will. But the rigid person's identification of himself with his will forbids recognition of the quality of his actual wishes as such and attenuates his experience of them to mere failures or lapses of will, often to some kind of "weakness" (an "addiction"; "inertia"; "something infantile in me").

The restriction of motivational experience implies a restriction, also, of objective consideration of the external situation or figure of interest. A selective picture is constructed in support of what the rigid person thinks he should do, a picture that omits all that accounts for his actual feelings, his wish, and often his action. It omits the actual attractions of the disapproved relationship, the relief offered by drinking, the unpleasant realities of the contemplated move.

In constructing this picture, the rigid person consults rules, "should's," where someone else looks at the situation; he asks himself, in the restaurant, what he should eat, when the next person thinks of the dishes on the menu; he applies the rule that no opportunity should be passed up, where the next person feels free to pick and choose, and looks things over accordingly; he thinks that no stone should be left unturned, where someone else sees clearly that further effort is pointless.

It is interesting to note that in this respect, in its absence of a clear, objective picture of the external figure or situation of interest, the rigidity of adult psychopathology is not different from the child's. The essential difference lies in the one case being an effect of the restrictions of psychological dynamics while the other is a reflection of limited cognitive capacity. Unlike the child's rigidity, however, pathological rigidity in the adult is intrinsically insecure and tense, because it is intrinsically ambivalent. Whereas, for the child, the rigid reliance on authoritative rules is basically in pursuit of his spontaneous interests, for the rigid adult that reliance is required to forestall anxiety, and overrules his spontaneous interests. Hence the rigid person's concern with self-control and "willpower." That concern with self-control becomes, then, an important value in itself. In this way, particular ramifications of general modes develop.

These individuals take pride in strength, in the specific sense of overcoming oneself, one's inclinations or wishes, and feel shame or contempt for what they regard as weakness, giving in to oneself, failing to overcome those inclinations or wishes. Strength or weakness of will becomes a measure, sometimes a critical measure, for self-respect. One's will, as distinct from his inclinations, is to one degree or another identified as the true and legitimate agent of one's actions ("something infantile in me wants to drink, but *I* don't want to"), and to that degree, feelings or wishes inconsistent with the will are recognized only as aberrations or, in the case of extreme rigidity, as the expression of an alien agency of some sort.

The person who can respect and even recognize in himself only what he thinks he "should" be, according to rules and images to which he can never totally conform, can have at best an exaggerated and uncertain self-respect and sense of mastery of himself. More likely, he will experience constant fluctuations of that self-respect and sense of mastery. We often see in such people a defensive haughtiness or even arrogance, but one that hardly forestalls a sense of inferiority and feelings of shame or humiliation. They may be quite conscious of status, attempting to dispel feelings of not being enough with reminders that they are more than others. Above all, they are in these ways self-conscious, continually watching, measuring, and evaluating themselves.

The symptoms and traits that I have described are characteristic in some form or degree of all the varieties of rigid character. It is not a comfortable style. Considering the discomfort that is intrinsic to these dynamics, in fact, one might easily wonder if the subjective cost of such a character organization does not outweigh its defensive benefit. That doubt, indeed, can be raised about psychopathology in all its varieties. But the turns and ramifications of psychological development are not planned and calculated for their ultimate result. They are reflexive reactions to immediate circumstances and sensations and each such turn can only start from the resting point of the last.

What follows considers the two principal forms of rigid character, obsessive-compulsive and paranoid. Despite the disparity in their respective symptoms, the relationship between obsessive-compulsive and paranoid conditions is, if anything, closer than the one described earlier between hysterical and psychopathic character. Not only is there a clearly defined relation between their respective symptoms and traits, but also the comparatively less rigid and more stable obsessive-compulsive condition may be the setting for the development of a more severe, less stable paranoid one. This fact suggests that the two conditions may represent not defensive adaptations of two closely related, but distinct, prevolitional modes, as in the case of hysterical and psychopathic character, but a single mode of rigidity that in some instances can take more extreme, less stable forms. In any case, we are not yet able to identify with any confidence the particular variety of obsessive-compulsive character, among many, that is susceptible to paranoid developments.

OBSESSIVE-COMPULSIVE RIGIDITY

"Rigid character," as described here, mainly refers to one or another form of obsessive-compulsive character. The obsessive-compulsive not only represents the predominant and most easily recognized rigid character; it is, also, in a certain sense, the most fundamental kind. That is to say the essential dynamics of rigid character are most easily visible in obsessive-compulsive conditions, and other symptoms or traits that are sometimes apparent in rigid character, such as sadism and masochism, are not difficult to derive from these dynamics (Shapiro, 1981). Paranoid conditions also may be considered a kind of transformation of obsessive-compulsive character.

It is in the well-known obsessive and compulsive symptoms that the loss, or the defensive avoidance, of agency and of a sense of personal motivation is dramatically clear. In the compulsive ritual of hand washing, for instance, the "reeling off" of behavior according to an inner program and without consideration of external realities is conspicuous. It is only slightly less conspicuous in the more general trait of obsessive perfectionism, a trait that is hardly removed at all from the child's prevolitional rigidity. The insistence that things be "just right," without distinction between the objectively important and the objectively trivial, dispenses with the normal act of autonomous judgment. The subjective sense of agency is replaced by a vague sense of being rule-driven.

Much the same point can be made about the more or less continuous purposefulness of obsessive-compulsive people. Obsessive purposefulness has a markedly different subjective quality from ordinary purposefulness. It is not an expression of a personal aim in the ordinary sense, a wish to do something or effect some change in relation to the external world. The impetus for obsessive-compulsive purposefulness comes not from the relationship between the individual and the external world but from his relationship to himself. Such purposefulness often has considerable realistic value, but it may consist nevertheless largely of doing for the sake of doing or, more precisely, doing for the sake of having done.

The extreme case of an effort to satisfy an internal directive of this kind is compulsive ritual, where the result may be no product or a product of no objective value whatever. But the distinction between compulsive ritual and ordinary compulsive purposefulness is not as sharp as might be thought; a good deal of purposeful activity of this kind—taking the briefcase home at night—is essentially ritualistic, although rationalized.

In ritual and only less acutely in ordinary compulsive purposefulness, the individual feels, in contrast to normal experience, like a servant of his purpose. He feels the responsibility that the dutiful soldier feels to satisfy military regulations, quite apart from whether he knows their reasons. The result of his effort, accordingly, may be the soldier's satisfaction with a duty done or shame at his failure and inadequacy. But in neither of these cases is there a sense of genuine self-direction or choice, except as the executor of assigned responsibility. The sense of duty, or of responsibility to superior authority, in this sense, dilutes the experience of personal choice and motivation, or supplants it in consciousness altogether, even while it intensifies the experience of failure.

Obsessive-compulsive rigidity is a rigidity of duty or, in a quite special sense, of conscientiousness. This conscientiousness is not merely, as it is often described, more harsh than the normal person's, or excessive. It is not like the normal conscience in greater degree, only more principled or more stringent. The most stringent moral principles are no sign of neurosis. The specialness of obsessive-compulsive conscientiousness is not a quantitative matter at all, but an essential difference of quality. It is a conscientiousness of rules, something quite different from a conscientiousness of personal conviction. A conscientiousness of rules dilutes or displaces the normal experience of personal choice and agency, whereas the ordinary conscience participates in that experience. That is why obsessively conscientious people including, for instance, obsessively religious people, may be capable of surprising moral transgressions. It is why obsessively clean people may allow themselves to be quite dirty in some ways.

This is not to say that an ordinary conscience, a conscience of conviction, is absent in obsessive people or that these people live only with a conscientiousness of rules. They may have a normal conscience, just as they may have normal judgment. It is only that in certain instances an additional, redundant, rule-based authority displaces that ordinary judgment or conscience. Quite apart from their rules, their should's and should not's, however, obsessive people, like other people, have values and principles that influence the way they see things, their everyday choices, and their less self-conscious actions. Although these values may be represented in much, perhaps most, of their activity, they are generally unnoticed, as one's values tend to be for most people; they are lenses through which one sees the world. But where choices and actions call attention to themselves, where decisions must be made that unavoidably raise consciousness of personal agency, obsessive individuals cannot rely on their own values or their own judgments without anxiety. They do not dare, at those times, to disregard their rules. This is evident even in mundane, objectively innocuous choices that call attention to themselves merely because they deviate from established, hence authoritative, routine.

When, for example, an obsessive man is tempted occasionally to interrupt his regular schedule of play sessions with the infant son to whom he is actually quite devoted, he anxiously evokes the specter of lasting damage to the child ("all the books say . . . "). The problem leads him to further anxieties. This very decent man worries that if he "just did what (he) wanted to do," he might become utterly indifferent to the needs and suffering of others, even of his own family. This is not merely a reflection of unconscious ambivalence; it is a construction prompted by his alarm at a deviation from rules.

Compulsive rituals, such as hand-washing rituals, checking the door lock repeatedly, and such, in which the rule-based nature of obsessive conscientiousness is especially clear, typically resemble—perhaps one should say simulate—precautionary or corrective acts, conscientious acts against mishap. But it is obvious, to a certain extent even to the obsessive person himself, that they do not reflect a conscientious judgment of the real world. They do not express a relationship between the doer and the external world at all, as normal motivation and action do, but are, again, actions done for the sake of doing them, or satisfying the doer that they have been done.

It follows from this aim that although such actions may be modeled after normal precautions or reasonable purposes, they are essentially formalistic, often exaggeratedly so. Sometimes their formalistic or ceremonial quality is quite inconspicuous, to the obsessive person himself as well as to others, on account of its resemblance to ordinary purposes: The businessman who carries his briefcase home every night tells himself that he does so "in case" he wants to work. But sometimes these actions have been rendered so remote from realistic purposes, by processes I shall describe, as to be impossible to rationalize. Such actions are conspicuous, and it is these that are generally recognized as symptoms.

If living under the authority of rules avoids anxiety, it also is inevitably oppressive. It requires a continual awareness of the existence of those rules, a continual awareness of should's. This is evident in the obsessive-compulsive person's continual reminding of himself, nagging of himself, that he "should" do this or that. His consciousness of rules has the effect of transforming them into demanding imperatives ("You *should do* . . . !"). Quite often these imperatives demand simply "You should do *more!*" The typical repetitive compulsive symptom is thus a particular form of the driven purposefulness of obsessive-compulsive people, of their general sense that they should be *doing*.

The corollary to the continual pressure *to do* is the prohibition of any extended satisfaction. That is to say, consciousness of oneself unaccompanied by a nagging supervision or by an awareness of any further should's is an anxious experience. Consciousness of such experience, or of a pause in purposeful *doing*, arouses in the obsessive individual anxious concerns of wasting precious time, missing opportunities, and such, and prompts a renewal of pressure to do. Indeed, consciousness of the momentary absence of such pressure may even prompt a searching of the mind for something that should be done, such as an unfulfilled responsibility or a concern that needs thinking about. Such a prompting constitutes a reminder of the requirement of purposeful doing even before any specific objective has been identified. For example, an obsessive man notices that after awakening in the morning, he "look(s) for something to worry about."

In short, the requirements of a rigid or rule-based conscientiousness can never be satisfied, can never permit extended satisfaction. However thorough or recent the hand washing, there is always the remaining possibility of incompleteness, of something overlooked, of some residual or newly acquired contaminant. Hence it is intrinsic to this kind of scrupulosity that it is relentless. It therefore happens, particularly under conditions of special anxiety, that obsessive conscientiousness tends to extend its domain. The man who worries about germs cannot overlook the possibility of HIV contamination. Contamination by food handlers who might have open wounds cannot be ruled out—restaurants, in particular, must be avoided—but neither can prepared food be exempted from concern; any red or reddish particles on such food might be blood; and so forth. The relentlessness and repetitiveness of obsessive concerns and their tendency to extend their domain are further symptomatic ramifications of the general rule-directed prevolitional mode.

The same principle that no possibility of concern should be overlooked sometimes leads to the turning of obsessive concerns back upon themselves. The man who is worried about infection, becoming aware of his anxiety, thinks he might be losing his mind, that he might then have to go to a mental hospital. Precautionary or corrective actions may also require their own precautions or corrections. Repeated checking of the lock leads to the concern that one may have damaged it, requiring a new start from the beginning.

Generally, however, these extensions of obsessive concerns have limits. The very fact that they are essentially rule-driven formalities, ceremonial simulations of precautionary or corrective actions, permits certain formal revisions of them. Procedures that threaten endless extension or repetition may be more or less satisfied by technical economies, such as a particular number or sequence of precautionary checks, or symbolic representations of the original actions, or other economic formulas.

The precautionary or corrective acts, or ceremonies, that constitute compulsive rituals in general may be transformed by legalistic extensions and technical economies into gestures increasingly remote from realistic judgment, and even remote from their original aims. Routines may acquire an authority of their own, the "rightness" of established procedure, from which no deviation can be tolerated without anxiety. In all of this, the original aims, ceremonial but still comprehensible, may easily be lost, as they often are in religious ceremony. Once again, in this way a general characterological reliance on a prevolitional rule-directed mode can ultimately branch into quite cryptic ritualistic symptoms.

The most common obsessive precautionary action is worry, a thought-action. To anticipate trouble, never to overlook any possibility of trouble, to keep such possibilities in mind, is doing something. Inasmuch as such precautionary thinking is necessarily biased, paying special respect as it does to the worst possibilities, its general effect is to live with the worst, even to assume the worst, as though in preparation for the worst.

In its more benign, less relentless, forms, this bias merely distorts realistic proportions. Often, however, new possibilities are discovered that require worry. Sometimes these are horrific, like the prospect of HIV contamination cited above. But sometimes they are only far-fetched concerns that clearly are not believed by the obsessive person himself, yet cannot conscientiously be dismissed.

> For example, an obsessive businessman arrives at his destination with the concern that a tree branch he "might have" driven over "could have" been flipped in the air, come down, and hurt someone, though no one was visible on the road. Maybe, he says, he had better check. He says this without conviction, and he makes no move to check.

These ideas do not reflect a true impairment of judgment, for the obsessive worrier does not actually believe in the troubles he imagines. His worries are typically full of "might be's," "could be's," and "maybe's." They are not judgments of reality at all. The obsessive person suspends his judgment of reality in favor of his rules of conscientiousness. It is for this reason that the man cited above does not look convinced that he really might have hurt someone. When it is suggested to him that he does not seem to believe that possibility is real, he avoids responding directly. "Maybe" he should check, he says, "just in case."

It is precisely because these obsessive ideas, although they displace judgment, are not themselves judgments in the ordinary sense that they can exist side by side with quite realistic judgment and behavior. The man who worries that he "might" have hurt someone on the road does not trouble himself to investigate; the person who seems frantic with worry that he might have AIDS may not even bother to have a blood test. (And if he does bother to do that, he does so not simply in the hope that he is well, for he may know that he is well, but largely to satisfy the technical precautionary requirement and thereby make it permissible to cease worrying.) Often, in other words, even ostensibly grave obsessive worries will give way to practical judgment where action is concerned.

Another kind of conscientious, precautionary action is the monitoring of oneself, of one's own mind, for scandalous ideas or terrible "impulses." The status of these thoughts or impulses is sometimes misunderstood psychiatrically when the obsessive individual's own worried or alarmed idea is taken at face value. It is important to recognize that these ideas or "impulses" arise in the mind of a person who is monitoring his thoughts with a relentless scrupulousness. These are people who, without realizing that they do so, watch, even search, their own minds with the zeal of a personal Inquisitor, and such a search cannot fail to bring results.

For example, a deeply religious, but obsessive man soberly reported that he had counted 142 "sinful thoughts" in a single day.

The horrific "impulses"—actually they are *ideas* of impulses—that the obsessive person sometimes believes he is struggling to control are not so different from other obsessive thoughts. Once the obsessive person, searching his mind, discovers these alarming ideas—that he "might" rape or kill an innocent child, or drive off a bridge, or shout something scandalous—he feels that he must pursue them, face, and admit to himself their worst implications. He feels, also, that he must continue to monitor his mind so that these or other impulses do not escape control. Thus one such man explained, after realizing that he searches his mind each morning for terrible thoughts, particularly thoughts about assaulting a young girl, that if he did not identify those thoughts, if he allowed himself to lose track of them, then he "might actually do it."

The content of these ideas or "impulses" is not necessarily without any basis in fantasy. But they have been exaggerated into alarming threats, if not largely constructed, by the zeal of a thought-monitor. These concerns, also, are full of "might's" and "could's," like other forms of obsessional worry.

They are precautionary concerns, aimed at rooting out dangers. They reflect, essentially, the rigid person's nervousness and distrust of his own unguarded action, action without rules.

The obsessive-compulsive symptoms and traits described are perhaps the most familiar and common ones. But variations of these symptoms and traits appear in a great many different varieties and contexts of obsessive-compulsive character. They may be conspicuous in an intensely driven individual of many accomplishments or in a quiet person driven less to accomplishment than to worrying. These character differences, about which we know little, are likely to involve differences in degree of rigidity, though they are not likely to be matters of degree of rigidity alone.

Difference in degree of rigidity may well be an important factor in the distinction between those forms of obsessive-compulsive character that may become settings for paranoid developments and the much larger group that will not. Most, seemingly less rigid, obsessive-compulsive individuals are quite conscious of *internal* conflict, even preoccupied by it; being more conscious of what they consider their own weaknesses and inadequacies, they are more likely to be wrestling with themselves, nagging themselves relentlessly, and worrying. Those who are more rigid, who have an exaggerated confidence in their strength of will, are more contemptuous of weakness, perhaps more dogmatic, and altogether more estranged from themselves. There is a certain theoretical justification, as will become clear in what follows, to the surmise that paranoid symptoms are more likely to develop in the latter group.

Apart from such variations of obsessive-compulsive character, the dynamics of rigid character may branch or extend in many directions, and obsessive-compulsive symptoms and traits are likely to be associated with any of those extensions. They are likely to be present, for example, in individuals with pronounced sadistic and masochistic traits, accompanied as those traits usually are by preoccupations with strength or weakness of will; with forcing the other to give in, or being forced; with disciplining or being disciplined (Shapiro, 1989). Paranoid conditions, whose close relation to the obsessive-compulsive we shall consider in more detail, are another such ramification of rigid character. And as the later chapters of this book will indicate, obsessive-compulsive features are commonly in evidence in at least two forms of schizophrenia. All this reflects, once again, that the usual psychiatric categories do not describe discrete diseases, but varieties of more general character forms.

Paranoid Rigidity

The kinship of obsessive-compulsive and paranoid attitudes and of the general form of their respective symptoms is especially striking, despite the disparity of symptom content and traditionally recognized defense mechanisms. The kinship is close enough to give the two conditions a similar "feel" in many respects. The compulsive individual's self-conscious measuring of himself seems a milder form of paranoid acute self-consciousness. There is the careful deliberateness of the one and the still more careful guardedness of the other; the anticipation of trouble that we call obsessive worrying and the paranoid anticipation of threat; the stubborn resistance to influence of the one and the suspicious resistance of the other.

The relationship goes further. We have already considered the kinship of the dogmatic attitudes common in compulsive character and paranoid knowingness. Even the paranoid delusion in its general quality as an anxious preoccupying idea stripped of realistic proportion may be said to resemble an extreme form of obsession. It is their formal relationship that is responsible for the difficulty, in certain cases, of establishing the differential diagnosis between paranoid and severely rigid, obsessive conditions, as well as for the occasional development of the one condition from the other.

In certain respects, the formal relation between obsessive-compulsive and paranoid rigidity can be defined rather precisely. It is evident that in every instance of comparison, the paranoid condition is the more rigid, but that is not the most striking feature of the relationship. Its most striking feature is the transformation of the obsessive-compulsive's struggle with himself into a corresponding experience in the paranoid case of conflict with an external antagonist. The correspondence is quite exact. Where the compulsive person experiences a conscious struggle against "giving in" to himself and against various kinds of weakness of will, the paranoid person experiences a struggle against external efforts to make him "give in," to subjugate or coerce him, to weaken his will or undermine his resistance. Where the compulsive person contends with feelings that he is less than what he should be, the paranoid person contends with external efforts to humiliate him and make him feel small. The rigid person's struggle to subjugate himself to his will is central to each condition. For the compulsive person it is experienced as such, as an effort to overcome his own weaknesses, whereas for the paranoid person its locus has shifted to the external world. This transformation implies a more complete estrangement of the individual from himself (See Table 2).

Self-estrangement in some form or degree is present in all psychopathology. It is evident in the obsessive-compulsive person's attempts to identify himself with what he thinks he should be and his repudiation of feelings or wishes that are contrary to his willful purposes and directives. It is most clearly evident in his recognition of those feelings or wishes only in the narrow and prejudiced terms of their failure to conform to his willful purposes, that is, only as aberrations, lapses, or weaknesses of will, as laziness, "inertia," or "something infantile in me." Yet, in these limited ways, he does recognize the existence of such feelings or wishes. If he does not recognize them fully as such, as his own feelings or wishes, he at least experiences them as his own lapses or weaknesses, or his own failure to be what he should be. Indeed, he repents such failures and insufficiencies, is conscious of his shame, and renews his nagging of himself and his reminders of what he should be.

In the paranoid case a greater underlying shame and contempt for the self has driven the rigid individual to a greater but less stable rigidity, to a more urgent but less successful repudiation of his subjective life. The subject of Freud's study of paranoia, Schreber, to take an extreme instance, utterly disavowed his female sexual fantasies with the indignant assertion that his own character was "morally unblemished"; he imagined, rather, that he was being transformed into a "female harlot" by an external agency (Schreber, 1955).

More commonly, paranoid individuals are driven simply to exaggerated assertions of will and authority, to the knowingness discussed earlier, to an inflated pride, even arrogance and sometimes grandiosity. That pride is extremely unsure, as one would expect of people who are trying to subdue feelings of inferiority and shame. Hence these people are highly sensitive to slights, indignities, or disrespect, alert to the possibility of humiliation. They are, in a word, defensive. Indeed, defensiveness is intrinsic to a rigidity of this kind and degree.

A person of rigid will must, after all, guard two fronts: He must guard against both the threat of external coercion and the threat of internal temptation. To put it another way, the rigid person must avoid two kinds of weakness: giving in to others and giving in to himself, to his own feelings and wishes. The two forms of weakness have, in that way, a subjective equivalence; to the rigid person they feel much the same, and a concern about one kind of giving in is never present without some degree of concern

TABLE 2 Rigid Modes

	Obsessive-Compulsive	Paranoid
Modes of Activity	Rule directed, rigid "will," purposeful, productive	Rigid self-control and defensive mobilization, guarded against efforts to weaken or coerce "will"
Sense of Agency	Identification with rigid "will" ("should's"), loss of clear sense of own wishes	Defensive identification with rigid "will," alienation from own wishes, concern with autonomy
Affect	Limited by constant purposefulness	Extremely limited by defensive mobilization; defensive anger
Relation to External Influence	Stubborn	Suspicious
Cognition	Purposeful, biased	Rigid defensive bias

about the other. There is, so to speak, a communication between the two fronts; an *internal* threat to the rigid will can, particularly in the case of extreme rigidity, easily be translated into a defensive sense of vulnerability on the *external* front. This relation between the two kinds of threat is the pivot on which the paranoid transformation of internal conflict into external conflict turns.

While it is true that the obsessive-compulsive person is primarily wrapped up in wrestling with himself, he is also well known for his stubbornness. That stubbornness corresponds, in its function of resisting external influence, to the hypersensitive and suspicious attitude of the paranoid. But the differences between the two attitudes, the comparative imperturbability of the one and the hypersensitivity of the other, reflect the difference between the two kinds of rigidity, particularly their relative stability, and reveal something of paranoid dynamics.

The compulsive person's stubbornness and imperturbability is a principled refusal to divert attention from his own purposes. It is on the whole supplementary to his determined, often productive purposefulness. He will not be diverted from those purposes either by himself or anyone else. In the paranoid context of a rigidity that is more extreme, under greater internal tension and less stable than the compulsive's, that relatively imperturbable refusal or dismissal of external influence is replaced by a defensive, often hostile anticipation of it. In the context of a more fragile internal structure, stubbornness is replaced by suspiciousness. Suspiciousness, one might say, is a stubbornness that has become more insecure, therefore defensive.

If the effort to subdue shame and what is shameful with exaggerated assertions of authority and will is fragile, external circumstances that challenge that authority or will are bound to be threatening. These are the circumstances to which paranoid people are extremely sensitive. Any treatment at the hands of another person or institution that may seem coercive or disrespectful, anything that resembles being "pushed around," any hint of indignity, condescension or rebuff, particularly by an admired figure or someone of superior rank whose appreciation is desired, will in effect remind the paranoid individual of his smallness, that is, will humiliate him and arouse his defensiveness.

> One such man, advised that he should address his superior at work as Mr.—, angrily denounced the idea, insisting that he would never "crawl."

Sometimes the mere presence of admired figures threatens indignity. Such admiration, therefore, is often grudging or denied, and those figures often become objects of prideful, defensive sensitivity and antagonism.

All this says that a defensive and antagonistic relationship with the external world, particularly with certain figures, is intrinsic to a rigid self-direction of this extreme and unstable sort. Defensiveness of this kind is central to paranoid character and is not, as sometimes has been thought, a secondary product of projected aggression. At the same stroke this kind of rigidity forestalls conscious awareness of shameful and repugnant feelings and replaces that self-awareness with an external target. In that sense, a stabilizing solution is found for an otherwise insecure rigidity. The defensive relationship that results is not one of an unspecific hostility or aggressiveness. That relationship is characteized specifically by the touchiness, the alertness to humiliation, the bitterness, and even the hatred that one who feels inferior or ashamed, but does not know it, harbors toward those he himself considers his betters.

The central defense mechanism in paranoid conditions has been thought to be projection, although neither its psychological basis nor its exact workings have been clear in the psychoanalytic literature. Actually, the phenomena of projection are fairly direct effects of paranoid defensiveness. Defensiveness of this kind, with its anticipation of threat, implies an extreme cognitive bias, a suspicious bias. The person who feels vulnerable cannot afford the luxury of openmindedness or balanced judgment. He searches only for signs of threat. The nature of that threat will be determined by the particular ways in which he feels vulnerable, and that sense of vulnerability will have been defined by those aspects of himself, those ideas or feelings, that he repudiates. The more anxious or unstable the paranoid individual is, the greater his defensiveness, and the more extreme and rigid his bias. Evidence that satisfies that defensive and unrecognized bias will be leaped at, its mitigating context brushed aside. With a sufficiently rigid and narrow bias, the discovery of a threat of humiliation, insult, or indignity, or an attempt at coercion or trickery or other subversion of the will is therefore inevitable. The outcome of this process is, in other words, the phenomenon of projection (See Table 3).

Projective ideas are not, therefore, as they commonly are described, direct reflections of abhorrent and repudiated unconscious feelings or motivations; *they are reflections of the defensive concerns to which those feelings or motivations*

TABLE 3 Obsessive-Compulsive and Paranoid Ramifications of Rigid Character

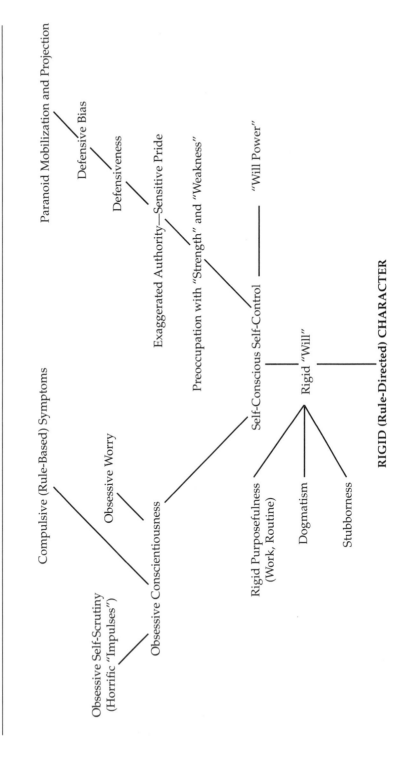

give rise. It is because those ideas are products of defensive anxieties and biases that their content is limited in its variety. The defensive concerns of one who feels ashamed are reflected in ideas of being watched, of humiliating exposure, of being seen as weak or effeminate, or in ideas of slights or insults to his status or authority. Anxieties about weakness of will, softness, or temptations to "give in" may give rise also to ideas of being coerced ("trapped") or subject to coercive or invasive influences (hypnosis, poisons) that weaken or undermine strength of will or, sometimes, its equivalent, bodily strength. The inevitable success of a sufficiently rigid and narrow bias in seizing on kernels of evidence and dismissing their context often confers an aura of confidence or knowingness, as described in Chapter 2, on projective ideas.

Rigidity and Passive-Reactiveness

The extreme case of paranoid rigidity helps to clarify the general relation of rigidity to passive-reactiveness, for here one sees them converge. As the paranoid defensive bias becomes increasingly rigid, judgment becomes increasingly immediate; genuine reflectiveness diminishes. The appearance of an intense and penetrating concentration in paranoid people often gives the impression of an effective, volitionally directed attention. But the inevitable "discovery" of the confirming clue makes it clear that the search is a rigid and exceedingly limited one, responsive only to an element that will satisfy expectation, and responsive to that element with an already more or less fixed idea. The more rigid and narrow the paranoid bias, the easier the identification of such an element becomes, and the more immediate the emergence of the final projective idea. In the extreme case of paranoid delusions, even the semblance of active searching disappears. The projective idea is triggered with such immediacy that all subjective sense and all external semblance of activeness is lost. The personally threatening message on the radio is *aimed* at the subject.

We shall return to this matter in the discussion of schizophrenia.

CHAPTER 6

Drivenness and Hypomania

There does not seem to be any precise or technical definition of "drivenness" in the psychiatric literature, but the term is commonly used and understood. It implies a more or less continuous activity, activity for its own sake, that seems to be urged or pressed internally, and of an intensity that cannot be relaxed without discomfort. Actually, we know that in the two familiar kinds of drivenness, obsessive-compulsive and hypomanic, any interruption of activity not only produces discomfort, but meets with conscious objection, regardless of the particular nature of the activity. The driven, compulsive individual becomes anxious and concerned that he is wasting time, "not doing anything." The hypomanic becomes irritated, sometimes angry, at interruption; his expansive mood is threatened or spoiled. This picture of driven activity shows it to be a defense, continually urged by the individual on himself to forestall discomfort.

In a general way, such a view of drivenness hardly distinguishes it from any other form of defensive, or anxiety-forestalling, process. Insofar as any defensive mode—the theatricality of the hysteric, say, or the impulsiveness of the psychopath—requires activity of some sort, that activity might reasonably be characterized as driven. But this particular defensive activity has certain distinctions: In particular, it includes an especially self-conscious urgency to *do*, and a far more explicit kind of *doing*.

Both obsessive-compulsive drivenneess and hypomanic drivenness forestall discomfort by activity, yet the respective qualities of their activity and of that discomfort are quite different. Obsessive-compulsive activity is highly purposeful, even disciplined, with a conscious aim to accomplish, particularly in measurable ways. Hypomanic activity, on the other hand, while ambitious, is typically far from disciplined. It consists largely of a driven spontaneity, an exaggerated immediacy of reaction. A rigid mode is defensively employed in the one case, a passive-reactive mode in the other. One might say that the drivenness of the obsessive-compulsive forestalls the discomfort of spontaneity by constant purposeful activity, while hypomanic drivenness forestalls the discomfort of reflectiveness with continuous "spontaneity."

HYPOMANIC DRIVENNESS

It remains to be shown, of course, that the hypomanic case actually is one of drivenness. After all, for many years, indeed long before the current biological trend in psychiatry, hypomanic and manic-depressive conditions have been widely accepted as biological rather than psychologically caused conditions. The reason often given for this assumption is the apparent absence of exciting psychological causes for these frequently episodic states.* As will be shown later, however, that absence of external and psychologically significant precipitants is by no means consistent. At any rate, although the supposed biological processes involved never have been precisely described, these conditions are commonly thought to have a biological "feel."

Various features, particularly of manic and hypomanic conditions, do seem plausibly to be direct effects of biological processes. Perhaps one reason that they, more than other kinds of psychopathology, have a biological "feel" is that, in a general way, they seem less ideational and are clearly more affective than other disorders. The euphoria, the intensity of excitement, the vaguely physical sensation of excitement that seems to presage the manic episode, the rapid flow—one might even say flood—of ideas and the general speeding-up of mentation, noticeable externally and experienced subjectively, are all easy to accept as biological effects. Indeed, common experience confirms that fluctuations of body chemistry can elevate mood. The normal sensation of physical well-being has such an effect, at times; the athlete's experience of "runner's high" is certainly an example; and the effects

---

*Freud mentions this reason for "the custom," already in 1922, of considering these cases other than psychogenic, but he proceeds nevertheless to offer an explanation in terms of psychological dynamics (Freud, 1922, 49).

of various drugs, even the mild elevation of mood produced by alchohol, confirm the susceptibility of mood to body chemistry. It is often argued, in fact, that manic and depressive episodes have a regular periodicity presumed to reflect biological fluctuations.

But there are also strong arguments on the other side. The most obvious of these arguments is simply that, however susceptible mood may be to biological conditions, it is certainly no less susceptible to psychological ones. We expect excitement and elation in someone who has fallen in love, to take an obvious example. The formerly manic patient, John Custance, makes just that comparison in his recollection of his own condition (Custance, 1952). As a matter of fact, inasmuch as such psychological reactions have at least temporary physiological effects, we have a demonstration that, as far as mood fluctuations are concerned, the relation between biology and psychology is not altogether in one direction.

There is, actually, ample evidence that certain situations can give rise in normal people to affective states that strikingly resemble hypomania (although those situationally induced states do not seem to last much beyond the situation itself). Freud, for example, leaning on LeBon's work (LeBon, 1896) in his discussion of crowd psychology (Freud, 1922/1949), pointed out that the experience and behavior of people in crowds, particularly at festivals, reflects a liberation from the usual restrictions of the "ego ideal" (or superego) of the kind one sees in mania.

Freud says that ". . . in a group the individual is brought under conditions which allow him to throw off the repressions of his unconscious instinctual impulses . . . We can find no difficulty in understanding the disappearance of conscience or of a sense of responsibility in these circumstances" (Freud, 1921/1955, p. 74).

There is no doubt that the liberation from personal responsibility that comes with action in a group can have the effect of excitement and elation. Indeed, LeBon describes the "crowd mind," its loss of moral inhibition and the normal restraints of reason (no trace of the "critical spirit") in terms very suggestive of such a liberation. LeBon's description of crowds also includes formal characteristics of thought and cognition ("immediate generalization"; "association of disunited things") remarkably like the hypomanic's.

Contemporary examples of comparable excitement and loss of inhibition at reunions or celebrations or, for that matter, group activities whose explicit aim is to abandon inhibition are not hard to find. The description of an episode of so-called wilding, in which a group of adolescents expressly set out to discard all restraints, that culminated in this instance in a brutal rape, suggests a hypomaniclike excitement. One of the participants described the scene: "Everyone laughed and was leaping around . . . everyone was acting stupid" (*The New York Times*, 11/4/89).

There are other considerations in favor of psychological causation as well. Despite claims, accepted by Freud himself, that manic episodes appear periodically without relation to psychologically significant events, there is considerable evidence, in many cases, of the existence of such precipitants. Thomas Freeman, for instance, reports a case of a manic episode triggered in a female patient by the appearance on the ward of a young attendant with whom she thought she was in love (Freeman, 1976). Perhaps more instructive is Clara Thompson's observation of the emergence of a hypomanic state in an initially depressed and self-reproachful patient after only a few weeks of psychotherapy with a sympathetic therapist (Green, 1964). It is my impression that an effect such as Thompson observed is not rare, and I, myself, have seen similar developments.

There is, it seems to me, one consideration above all that decisively answers the question of whether manic or hypomanic episodes, or the depressive ones with which they are typically associated, can be purely biological: These conditions give strong evidence of internal conflict; they contain psychological dynamics. It is easy enough to understand that a mood or general feeling state can be directly influenced chemically or physiologically, but it is not at all easy to imagine the chemical creation of psychological dynamics.

DYNAMICS

The manic-depressive John Custance offers a glimpse of those dynamics. It confirms Freud's supposition. Custance says, of his depressed periods, "I am haunted by a sense of guilt; my conscience gives me no rest . . . Whatever I am doing, I feel I ought to be doing something else. I worry perpetually about past sins and failures . . . " (Custance, 1952, p. 61) while, by contrast, "In mania (the burden of conscience) is lifted as if by magic" (Custance, p. 50).

Manic or hypomanic conditions, and depression, as well, for that matter, are not simply "mood disorders." Hypomanic states do not consist only of sensations of excitement and feelings of elation. That excitement and elation have ideational content, and that content embodies specific anxiety-forestalling attitudes. Those defensive attitudes are, in fact, sometimes consciously articulated. One might almost speak of a hypomanic ideology, a program that defines the principles of hypomanic drivenness. It is, above all, a program of determined spontaneity, of immediacy of reaction, of rejection of second thoughts, hesitation, and constraint, even of reflection, reason, and judgement altogether as constraining (Custance, p. 174). It is doubtless that determination that regularly conveys to the clinical observer the impression that hypomanic euphoria is ungenuine or pretended. As Custance puts it, the aim is to achieve "the freedom to do what we like, the freedom of the released Id . . . freedom from laws, restraints, inhibitions of all kinds" (p. 145).

It is true that most often this freedom is described not as a program but simply as an extraordinary experience. The burden of conscience seems simply to be "lifted as if by magic." But the evidence indicates that this experience is not achieved or sustained without activity. This is particularly apparent when the euphoria begins to fade. The formerly manic journalist, Alonzo Graves, remarking on the fragility of his elation, speaks explicitly of the necessity to maintain it actively. He observes, "The euphoria . . . succumbs most quickly to the continuous pricking of the reality, and will require some deliberate summoning. . . . Personally, I have often sung to make myself feel cheerful . . . " (Graves, 1942, p. 673).

It is apparent that the activity must be of a sort that forestalls self-critical thought. In particular, according to Custance, it means "a state of constant activity"; "above all, staying 'on the move'" (quoted in Podvoll, 1990, p. 76).

The forestalling of self-critical thought may require the avoidance of critical thought altogether. Thus, Custance advocates the rejection of the "normal inhibitions of reason," and he sometimes attempts to sustain his spirits by, among other activities, "automatic writing," writing rapidly while avoiding attention to what is written. (The technique was employed by the surrealists in an effort to gain access to the unconscious; also, in other words, to liberate themselves from the constraints of conscious reflection.)

The psychoanalytic understanding of mania and hypomania emphasizes the defense mechanism of denial or "denial by overcompensation" (Fenichel, 1948, p. 410). The denial of self-critical or depressive ideas with a forced, compensatory optimism or self-congratulations ("Last night I was gorgeous!") is certainly present even in mildly hypomanic individuals. But this would seem to be of a piece with the more general defense mode of driven activity and the effort to avoid self-critical thought and the "constraints of reason." It seems likely that it is that driven activity and its avoidance of self-critical thought that makes it possible to avoid the "pricking of the reality" and to deceive oneself that the world is as one wishes it to be.

Perhaps, also, it is such activity that can generate, at least in certain individuals, a genuine sensation of excitement or "speediness," somewhat like a "runner's high," that lends support to the self-deception.

HYPOMANIA AND PSYCHOPATHIC CHARACTER

It seems paradoxical, but hypomania has been likened both to obsessive-compulsive conditions and to psychopathic ones. Actually, both comparisons are understandable (and I shall return to the obsessive-compulsive one later), but the relation to the psychopath is probably the more obvious. The essential defensive mode of the psychopath is, after all, an impulsive reactiveness, a quick reactiveness that avoids reflection. It is no accident, therefore, that exaggerations, often extreme exaggerations, of all the well-known traits of the psychopath—the lack of inhibition, the comparative fearlessness, the egocentricity, the glibness, the opportunism, as well as the reckless impulsiveness itself—can be found in the hypomanic person (see Table 4).

It is precisely the fact of this exaggeration that defines the hypomanic state, for it reflects the drivenness of that state. As a consequence of that drivenness, however, hypomanic traits are not merely exaggerations of the corresponding traits of the psychopath. The relation is more complicated than that. The hypomanic traits, however much they share with the corresponding psychopathic ones, are self-conscious in ways that the psychopathic traits are not. They are conspicuously effortful and artificial, consistently striking observers as "ungenuine" or "pretended" (Fenichel, 1948), unlike their corresponding numbers in the psychopath.

Thus, while psychopaths may be quite engaging socially, in a practiced, but easy, way, hypomanic individuals often issue a stream of jokes and entertainments. Psychopaths are uninhibited, often impulsive, sometimes reckless. The hypomanic is not just more impulsive—that, certainly, is so—but he is also consciously determined not to hesitate, consciously determined not to be deterred ("I'm going to do whatever I like!" [Freeman, 1976, p. 38]). The psychopath, in his impulsiveness, is relatively fearless. It is not simply that the hypomanic is more so; his *program* includes fearlessness ("Nothing is impossible!"). While the psychopath is glib, the hypomanic is even more facile with off-the-cuff ideas or utterances. He consciously rejects any need for second thoughts and asserts the right to do so.

99

TABLE 4 Hypomania and Psychopathic Character

	Passive-Reactive: Impulsive-Psychopathic	Driven Passive-Reactive: Hypomanic
Mode of Activity	Reckless, erratic, "spontaneous"	Pressured, reckless, hyperspontaneity
Sense of Agency	Diminshed sense of responsibility, externalization, "irresistible impulse"	Sense of being flooded by ideas and impulses; action feels effortless
Social Behavior	Uninhibited, sometimes engaging	Driven entertaining, forced spontaneity
Social Relations	Egocentric	Imperious
Conscience	Conscience faint, sense of responsibility avoided by quick action	Avoidance of self-criticism by forced spontaneity; sometimes interrupted by depression

> The Rorschach tester asks what made the inkblot look "bright and lovely"; the hypomanic patient replies, "Because I wanted it to be!" (Schafer, 1954, p. 254).

There is a further, quite important, but rather problematical expression of the hypomanic mode of forced and self-conscious spontaneity. It is the subjective experience of the spontaneity itself. Despite the evidence of the kind that I have cited that his spontaneity is forced and self-conscious, the hypomanic person experiences himself, at some point, as passively swept into action by a "flood" of ideas and impulses.

Even Custance, while describing his driven program at one point, at another speaks of the experience of "irresistible impulses coming from outside my (conscious) self." He says, "I can look at nothing without receiving some idea from it leading to an impulse to action" (Custance, 1952, p. 36).

The manic patient Graves, according to his hospital report, was more extreme and more explicit on this point (1942, p. 504). He is described as writing articles "without any mental effort . . . whatsoever. This made him wonder if his mind was not a transmitting device."

At first look, this passive experience of action seems, if anything, to confirm the simple biological theory of manic and hypomanic conditions. It suggests, in other words, not so much a picture of a hyperspontaneity driven by the individual himself as one that is driven by a biologically generated surge of energy that the individual must dispose of.

Here one must remember, however, that a diminished experience of agency is an aspect of every form of psychopathology, both passive-reactive forms and rigid forms. Wherever there is an abridgement of volitional processes, there is, also, a loss of experience of intentionality or agency, and the greater that attenuation of volition, the more extreme that subjective effect will be.

In particular, this loss of the subjective experience of agency is conspicuous in the impulsive psychopath, who is also "on the move." The psychopath is alert to opportunities for gain and quick to translate them into action, but he is hardly conscious of the intentionality contained in that alertness, or even of the intentions that prompt his actions. On the contrary, he is likely to tell us that the opportunity, or the temptation, simply presented itself ("As soon as I get out, somebody shoves a gun in my hand"), that the action that followed was invited, even required, by the circumstances ("He resisted"), or was driven by some irresistible internal force ("It was . . . all that stress" [Martin, 1991]; "The frustration gushes over" [Hevesi, 1991]).

One has only to imagine a driven intensification of this kind of reactiveness to arrive at the hypomanic experience of speedy action. For the psychopath, it is not he who deliberately initiates the action; it is the situation that "gets the adrenaline going" and triggers the idea and the action at the same stroke. For the hypomanic, driven to still speedier and unhesitating reactiveness, with its proportionally diminished awareness of agency and its undoubtedly greater physical sensation of excitement, the "adrenaline" is more powerful, and his experience is of a remarkable, barely containable "gushing over" of ideas and possibilities.

HYPOMANIA AND OBSESSIVE-COMPULSIVE CHARACTER

I have mentioned that a relationship of hypomania has been noted not only to psychopathic character, but also to the obsessive-compulsive. There is a good deal of clinical evidence, starting with the early days of psychoanalysis, to support the idea of such a relationship (Abraham, 1924/1953). Obsessive and compulsive symptoms and characteristics are often reported in manic-depressive individuals, particularly in connection with the depressive episodes.

John Custance, for instance, describing his frame of mind during a depressed period, says, "Whatever I am doing I feel I ought to be doing something else. I worry perpetually" (Custance, 1952, p. 61). It is typical obsessive experience. Custance mentions his performance of precautionary obsessive rituals, as well, in order, as he says, to propitiate Satan: "Every night I said the Lord's prayer backwards, letter by letter, smoking three ritual cigarettes as I did so . . . " (pp. 70–71). Indeed, in Custance's case, at least, the depression itself seems to be a product of a severe and relentless—that is, an obsessive—self-criticism. He says, for instance, ". . . my conscience gives me no rest . . . Not for a moment can I forget the mess I seem to have made of my life."

Much the same holds for the manic-depressive Alonzo Graves. He speaks of having "always lived in criticism of self" and of his "self-loathing" (Graves, 1942, p. 689). Indeed, one sees the direct expression of that self-loathing, and the rigid character's contempt for weakness, when he refers to his "cowardice" in fleeing from responsibility, his "despicable" crying (becoming "lacrymose"), and such (p. 144).

Obsessive characteristics, however, are not limited in these individuals to depressive periods. In fact, during the more "normal" periods, when they are neither acutely depressed nor clearly hypomanic or manic, they often show obsessive-compulsive traits and symptoms. Graves, for example, whose style of writing is in fact quite pedantic, speaks of himself as "a pedantic stoic man," "somewhat pompous." His idea of the "conscious mind" was one that is "disciplined, balanced and hard-working" (p. 665).

It is that last adjective, "hard-working," that is of special interest. For an obsessive-compulsive drivenness seems often to precede hypomanic or manic states. For example, Graves, a journalist, repeatedly refers to his ambitiousness ("tremendously ambitious") prior to his breakdown, and his efforts ("great enough to overstrain [his] capacities") to achieve his "life objectives" (p. 608). He speaks of the great pressures of his work, of the demands for exertion and concentration, of being "speeded up" (p. 178) by the requirements of work, and of finally becoming frantic.

It appears that a drivenness of an obsessive kind may be converted into a drivenness of a hypomanic kind. Graves, in fact, tells us: "Each [manic excitement] has been preceded by a commonsense effort, a straining for expression in writing, a concentration gradually passing into irrationality" (pp. 325–326). Referring to one occasion, in particular, when he is required to take on a great deal of extra work at his newspaper, Graves observes that in the course of such an effort, he experiences at a certain point the "realization of second and third powers of endurance which determination can tap . . . The expressional flow always betters for me in this phase" (p. 132).

It may be that a highly demanding or driven work-activity, under conditions where the necessity for speedy action makes hesitation or second thoughts impossible or irrelevant, can, at a certain point and for certain people, generate a sensation of easy and spontaneous production ("expressional flow").* If this is so, a transition from a burdened and effortful drivenness, a drivenness whose impetus and burden is a sense of responsibility, to a eu-

---

*Dr. Andreas Evdokas has attempted with some success to reproduce such an effect in normal subjects experimentally. By pressing his subjects for fast production on the Rorschach inkblot test, for example, he obtained such responses as "whirling dervishes"; "a highspeed plane"; "a rocket ship going up"; "two people . . . real excited"; "smoke bursting up" (Evdokas, 1997).

phoric hypomanic drivenness in which that burden is escaped, may be achieved.

Actually, the hypomanic state itself still bears marks of obsessive drivenness. It is often characterized not simply by grandiose ideas of any kind but, more specifically, ideas of great, usually beneficial, accomplishments such as bringing East and West together or liberating people from sexual constraints. Hypomanic ideas of that sort have been likened to obsessive-compulsive reaction formations (Fenichel, 1945), as in overdone acts of generosity. Nor, as we have seen, is hypomania a state merely of elation or cheerful excitement but, rather, one of *doing*, of great, ostensibly effortless, production, often imagined to be enormously creative as well.

> A mildly hypomanic man, emerging from depression, who had for years unsuccessfully attempted to complete a book, now says exultantly, "I don't have to write a novel! My life is a novel!"

All this strongly suggests that the agitated and obsessive self-criticism and nagging of the self (". . . Whatever I am doing, I feel I ought to be doing something else . . . ") that characterizes the depressive state in these individuals is by no means completely absent in the hypomanic state. It may be only momentarily and partially evaded with a type of compromise ("My life is a novel!"). In any case, the existence of a relation between the two kinds of drivenness is not hard to understand. They are, after all, two ways to forestall self-critical judgment and self-reproach by continuous *doing*, particularly *achieving*, either by hard work, in the one case, or inspired "spontaneity" in the other.

There is something more to be said about this curious relation between the psychopathic-like hyperspontaneity of the hypomanic state and the compulsiveness that seems to be visible in its background. What seems at first a peculiar combination of two defensive modes in a single condition may be taken as an example of their hierarchical organization in pathological character. Defensive modes are sometimes more and sometimes less successful. If a rigid and compulsively driven person suffers the relentless self-reproaches of a failure, perhaps in special circumstances, to satisfy the standards he has imposed upon himself, a further defensive reaction aimed at escaping these reproaches may be triggered. But, if our thinking is correct, this can only be a defensive reaction available to a person of driven character and a product of his ways and attitudes. One such possibility, perhaps available to some persons of that character, may be an effort to escape those driven and relentless self-reproaches by an equally driven heedlessness.

BIOLOGY

What can be said, finally, about the role of biology in such driven character, or specifically in hypomanic states? It is still not obvious that we should regard that role as essentially different from the role of biology in any other kind of psychopathology or, for that matter, any other aspect of human psychology. Obviously, human biological processes are basic conditions for human mentation and psychology in general. There is no doubt that individual biological variations and their developmental expressions will have psychological effects and will, for example, offer opportunities for defensive employment and therefore influence the form of psychopathology, if psychopathology should develop. On this account, it is unwarranted to assign responsibility for *any* psychopathology entirely to external circumstances if doing so implies that similar circumstances would have affected an individual of any biological constitution in the same way. If it should turn out that the biologically constituted affective system or general level of activity in individuals who develop manic or hypomanic and depressive conditions has predisposed them to these reactions, that would not be remarkable. But that is quite different from regarding those conditions as essentially independent of psychology.

SECTION THREE
NEUROSIS AND PSYCHOSIS

CHAPTER 7

Neurosis and Psychosis

We have accumulated so many facts about psychosis, particularly schizo-phrenia, both from clinical observation and more recently from biological and experimental studies, yet our understanding is far from satisfactory. For example, we know that it emerges sometimes gradually, sometimes acutely and with apparent abruptness, yet the psychological processes involved in its onset are not at all clear and have been understood in widely different ways. Indeed the whole relation of psychosis to nonpsychotic pathology is by no means settled. Do certain kinds of psychosis emerge from particular nonpsychotic conditions? Is the difference between psychotic and nonpsy-chotic pathology only one of degree, as certain continuities between them might suggest, or is there a fundamental qualitative difference between them? If the latter, what precisely is that difference? Is it the case, as Freud said, that neurosis is a turning away from internal conflict, while psychosis is a turning from the external world? Does the onset of schizophrenia repre-sent a failure and disruption of existing neurotic defenses, with the emer-gence of more primitive (and therefore often incomprehensible) ideation and affect or, as some say, is the schizophrenic's incoherence itself a defense, a way of warding off human contact?

Finally, of course, there is the question of the biological contribution to schizophrenia. In what follows, I will assume the existence of some biologi-cal and genetic predisposition. Such a predisposition may even be a neces-sary condition for schizophrenic symptoms, but in any case it does not seem a sufficient one. The questions remain therefore of the psychological structure and dynamics of schizophrenia. These questions have to some extent been put aside in recent years, but the assumption of a biological predisposition by no means disposes of them.

On the whole, we have a much clearer idea of the structure and dynamics of neurotic pathology than of psychosis, and that fact prompts the content and the organization of this chapter and the next. These chapters involve a comparative undertaking. I propose to make use of our understanding of neurotic, or nonpsychotic, conditions in order to clarify, first, the relation of those conditions to psychosis, and then to consider the nature and dynamics of psychosis—specifically schizophrenia—itself.

I want to examine, or reexamine, certain formal aspects of the *neurotic* person's relationship with the *external* world. The formal quality of that relationship, in contrast to the schizophrenic's relationship with the external world, has generally not been a focus of psychiatric interest. The neurotic's psychiatric problems are considered to be essentially problems of his relationship with himself. That much, I think, is correct. What is not correct is the further inference that his judgment of external reality is essentially realistic and, with the exception of particular figures or situations, his experience of the external world and his reactions to it are unremarkable. Indeed, the neurotic's "good contact with reality" is usually regarded as the essential factor that distinguishes his pathology from psychosis. But the facts are more complicated.

Close examination will show that the fundamental dimensions of the schizophrenic's impaired relationship with the external world are to be found in the neurotic's case as well, although in more moderate degree, of course. The general loss of an objective relation to reality, the impairment of the sense of self and consequently weakened "ego boundaries," the degradation of the quality of emotional experience, and finally, of course, the impairment of volitional self-direction that has been central to our discussion so far—all these are conspicuous and well known in their extreme forms in schizophrenia, and they are present more moderately in nonpsychotic pathology as well. In fact, they are symptomatic of psychopathology in general.

Formal symptoms of these kinds tend to be overlooked in neurotic conditions because the study of neurotic conditions has traditionally focused on the content of particular conflicts. However, such symptoms become conspicuous from a characterological perspective. I will review our understanding of the nature and the dynamics of these dimensions of the neurotic person's relationship with the external world, with the prospect of applying that understanding to the case of schizophrenia. I want to make clear, however, that finding a certain correspondence between the formal characteristics of neurotic and psychotic conditions, as I expect to do, does not imply that the distinction between neurosis and psychosis is only a matter of degree. It is obvious that there are critical dissimilarities between the two. But nature has its dialectics, and a change in degree often becomes at some point a change in kind.

The psychoanalytic understanding of psychosis, and following that the general psychiatric understanding, has been muddled by certain theoretical problems, especially problems arising from the traditional conception of defense. That conception, of defense mechanisms as impulse-controlling devices, has given rise to the idea of psychosis as a radical failure or disruption of neurotic defenses, a "decompensation," to use the common psychiatric term, and a regression to an earlier and more primitive state. Thus, in the conventional psychoanalytic view:

" . . . 'the dissolution of mental life which occurs during an acute psychotic attack brings about the complete disorganization of the ego. Only in a second phase is the ego reconstructed . . . New types of defense mechanism are created . . . of a completely different order from the defenses which . . . were effective during the pre-psychotic phase'" (Thomas Freeman, referring particularly to the formulations of M. Katan and others, 1981, p. 448).

But this picture of a "dissolution of mental life" or a "complete disorganization" of the ego, even in the acute phase of the onset of psychosis, is an inadequate description of a process of psychological change. What may appear to be a dissolution must in fact be a reorganization of mental life, and that reorganization must be determined by principles already inherent in that mental life. Indeed the very existence of a subsequent phase, a phase of reconstruction, implies a continuity of some sort.

In other words, if the regulatory system of an organization does fail in some sense or other and undergoes reorganization, it must do so according to the possibilities inherent in the nature of that system. And if this is so, one might think that the newly reorganized mental life will be characterized by a structure that has at least some definable relation to the original one, if not some actual continuity with it.

I want to propose such an understanding of the relation of nonpsychotic to psychotic conditions, and of the processes involved in the onset of psychosis, at least of schizophrenia. According to that understanding, the emergence of schizophrenia does not reflect a breakdown of characteristic anxiety-forestalling processes, processes of defense, but rather a radical extension and exaggeration of them. Many of the symptoms of schizophrenia are, of course, distinctive, but a kinship of their general forms with prepsychotic pathology can nevertheless be discerned.

This view of the nature of psychosis and its onset is suggested, actually, by the characterological nature of defense processes, as described in Chapter 3. The recognition that defense processes consist of general, characteristic anxiety-forestalling attitudes and modes makes it plain that those processes do not involve only the individual's internal relationship with himself, but invariably involve, at the same time, his relationship with external reality. All the anxiety-forestalling restrictions of motivational and emotional experience that we see in neurotic conditions are accompanied by restrictions and distortions of the relationship with external reality. These include general and systematic distortions of cognition and judgment.

Indeed, as will become clear in what follows, defensive restrictions of motivational and emotional experience can hardly be imagined without corresponding distortions of cognition and judgment. Furthermore, these nonpsychotic distortions of the individual's relationship with the external world reveal themselves on careful examination to be more moderate versions of the sorts of impairments and reality distortions otherwise familiar to us in psychotic conditions. It does seem, therefore, that the nature and dynamics of these neurotic symptoms can teach us something about their more extreme and more obscure psychotic forms.

It will be helpful, for our purposes, to review first some familiar facts about both neurotic and psychotic conditions.

NEUROTIC LOSS OF REALITY

Consider once again the example of an obsessional concern cited in Chapter 5. It manifests a striking loss of reality, as is not unusual in many such obsessional concerns, yet it seems clearly not to be psychotic:

A man arrives at an office that happens to be on a road bordered by trees. He looks worried, as he usually does, and at once explains anxiously that he has driven over a tree branch in the road, that the wheel of the car "might have" flipped the branch in the air, and that it "could have" come down somewhere and hurt someone. He adds that "maybe" he should go back and check. However, he makes no move to leave. Instead, he glances in a questioning way at the listener. Finally, he says, as if in apology for his concern, "Just in case." He seems to mean by this that he must take the idea that he may have been responsible for such an accident seriously, whether it is reasonable or not, whether he believes in it or not, as long as it is even remotely possible.

The obsessively conscientious attitude expressed by this person directly affects his judgment of reality. To be more precise, his idea does not represent a judgment of reality at all; it is a construction of that obsessive conscientiousness that might better be described as an *alternative* to a judgment of reality. He might rationalize his idea, as obsessive people sometimes do, as no more than carefulness, but in fact his attitude is not one of carefulness in the ordinary sense. Genuine carefulness springs from a concern to avoid error. But he is concerned only about the possibility of error in one direction, underestimation of his moral responsibility, and to avoid any such possibility, he distorts reality.

This one-sided concern constitutes a radical cognitive bias. No possibility of personal error or fault that comes to this obsessive person's mind can be dismissed, no matter how remote or even preposterous it may be, and however little the individual himself may be convinced of its reality. Actually, an obsessive conscientiousness often goes further. Even when no such possibility of fault presents itself spontaneously, it must be sought; the mind must be searched for it. An absence of evidence of fault cannot exclude the possibility of fault; it only prompts further, more searching, investigation. In this biased soul-searching, only a discovery of possible fault or personal error can be conclusive.

Obviously this process is different from the normal process of judgment or evaluation of reality. The direct relationship that normal judgment involves between the person and the external matter of interest encounters a complication here. An internal, essentially moral supervision and direction interferes with the normal subject-object relationship. According to this internal direction, certain ideas about reality must be given respectful consideration, even "belief," while other ideas or conclusions are prohibited. Ordinary judgment is in this way encumbered, to some extent even deflected, by a system of internal thought control. This restrictive process is an instance of what might be called the dynamics of obsessive bias or, perhaps in more general terms, the psychopathology of judgment.

These cognitive dynamics will, of course, affect judgment over a broad range of circumstances with similar results. The obsessively dutiful person will feel obliged in general to pay special respect to the disturbing possibility, the possibility of trouble or calamity, while temptation to credit the less troublesome possibility will be disdained as foolish and irresponsible ("the easy way out"). Consequently he will assume the worst. This distortion of reality is the general cognitive foundation of the most common of all obsessive symptoms, obsessive worry, as well as a great variety of other precautionary or corrective compulsive symptoms.

But can the thought-products of these dynamics really be called a distortion or loss of reality? Granting the existence of an obsessive bias of the sort described, it easily can be argued that the obsessive person still has distance from his own distortions of reality, and that it is precisely this distance, or capacity for reality testing, that distinguishes his case from psychosis. It is just the point, after all, that the obsessive person cited above does not say that he *has* hurt someone but only that he "might have." And it is precisely because he does not actually believe that he did, that he does not go back to the scene, but hopes instead for reassurance.

The evidence for the intactness of reality testing in such cases is not, in fact, usually limited to the qualifying "might have's" or "could be's," common as those locutions are in the language of obsessive worries. There is often the further evidence of action, or inaction, as there was in this case. Even the worrying student, who declares emphatically and in the language of conviction that he is sure he has failed his final examination and will be expelled, does not actually pack his bags. Sometimes obsessive worriers will even agree that they "worry too much." They may even say that a particular worry or obsessive idea is far-fetched, that they know perfectly well that it is "crazy." All these things are so, yet this matter of "distance" or "reality testing" is not so easily settled.

The fact is that the obsessive person's relationship with external reality cannot be measured along such a simple dimension as distance or reality testing. The processes involved are too complicated for that. It is quite true that the obsessive distortion of reality does not reflect any impairment, in the sense of damage, of cognitive faculties. We know that much, if only from the fluctuations in the extent of those distortions; an obsessive individual's worrying, for example, sometimes becomes more exaggerated, sometimes less, sometimes disappears. But it is also true that if his judgment is not impaired, it is at times quite unavailable to him. His dutiful attitudes may make it impossible for him to credit that judgment or even to recognize it, or articulate it to himself, if it is inconsistent with those attitudes. He may not dare—to put it better, it feels daring to him—to say or even to seriously think, "No, I am sure I did lock the door." The "might be's" and "could be's" of obsessive worries do reflect something less than belief, but in their insistent presence they express, also, a prohibition of a final disbelief. It is for this reason that the obsessive person's statements of apparent detachment, "I worry too much" or "I know it's crazy," however emphatic they may be, are never wholehearted. "I know it's crazy" is likely to be revised to "It's probably crazy" and then, "But who knows? Maybe . . . "*

In sum, the obsessive person does not know what he believes; his attitude fluctuates with the moment-to-moment internal dynamic situation. At one moment the dynamics of his character require him to suspend the ordinary act of judgment in favor of the possibilities of personal fault, error, or misfortune. At another moment, or perhaps even the same moment, the presence of a simpler, more genuine judgment of reality may reveal itself in action or even, perhaps faintly, in consciousness.

Louis Sass, in his valuable book *Madness and Modernism,* has called attention to the phenomenon sometimes observable in schizophrenics that he calls "double bookkeeping" (Sass, 1992). The schizophrenic patient who asserts a delusional identity, say of Jesus Christ, is yet likely to behave on the hospital ward like an ordinary citizen. Indeed, anecdotes are plentiful, among those who have spent some time with hospitalized schizophrenic patients, of the more or less normal behavior of these patients at times of emergency or other special occasions.

Sass argues that the attitude of the schizophrenic toward his delusion is not one of belief but a "suspension of disbelief." We shall return later to the question of that attitude in the schizophrenic, but such a characterization seems entirely apt for the case of the obsessive person. Of course, as in real double bookkeeping, the two accounts of reality do not have equal status;

---

*See the case of obsessive regret described in the last chapter of my book *Psychotherapy of Neurotic Character* (Shapiro, 1989).

there is the more acceptable, public account and the hidden, realistic one, in this case not even easily acknowledged by the subject to himself.*

The distortions of reality, or biases of judgment, on the part of suspicious people are very much like those I have just described in the obsessive case, although they are usually stated with comparatively more conviction. For people who feel vulnerable, an error of underestimating the possibility of threat is far more serious than its overestimation. Hence their bias toward an assumption of threat. But the suspicious person, like the obsessive, is not necessarily convinced of the realistic justification of his concern. He is convinced only that he must not neglect or underestimate its possibility, that he must not allow himself to be caught off guard, and therefore that he must not allow himself to believe he is safe. In both the obsessive and the suspicious cases, therefore, the distortions of reality are not reflections of cognitive damage, but of cognitive restrictions. The rigid bias of these pathologies, enforced by their dynamics, does not allow an objective relationship with external reality or a genuine judgment of reality, even while it freely permits fantastic worries and suspicions.

In other kinds of nonpsychotic pathology, restrictions of cognitive attitude distort reality in different directions. Consider, for instance, the impulsive and opportunistic individuals whose anxiety-forestalling spur-of-the-moment mode of action precludes serious planning and reflection. Sometimes these people are described as "indifferent to the future." It is more likely, however, that they avoid serious contemplation of the future than that they are actually indifferent to it. They frequently expect quick gain and entertain vague hopes, but they are oblivious of predictable risks and costs.

> For example, a hapless young man, already facing charges of petty crimes, is charged additionally with using the event of a hurricane to fake, with the help of his girlfriend's report, his own drowning and disappearance. When they *both* disappear, the police are, of course, alerted and they are quickly caught (Herszenhorn, 1998).

---

*The dynamics of such a "double bookkeeping," much as I have described them in the obsessive case, are revealed with remarkable clarity in the extraordinary memoir of John Perceval, written more than 150 years ago, describing his experience of psychosis. Referring to his delusional "voices," Perceval writes, "I perished from an habitual error of mind, common to many believers . . . because we force ourselves to say we believe what we do not believe, because we think doubt [of the "voice's" message] sinful" (Bateson, 1961).

Indeed, impulsive people often seem hapless. The person who avoids planning cannot have a realistic idea of the relation of present action to its distant consequences. It is a setting that makes wishful thinking easy. Even when costs arrive that are easily predictable to others, these people typically think of themselves simply as unlucky.

A loss of reality of yet another kind is evident in hysterical character. These individuals, with no confidence in their own authority, shrink from independent critical judgment. They are suggestible, their ideas are typically received ideas. Their judgments are usually conventional because they are unquestioning of public opinion ("He says . . . ", "Everybody says . . . "). Often they do not dare to credit their own perceptions.

> For example, a young woman, rebuked by her husband, a professor, for her distress at his attentions to pretty and admiring female students, now shamefacedly describes her own upset as "superneurotic." "He says," she explains, that he was only doing his job, and "he's right, it *is* part of his job." Only later, as she continues to talk about the incident, does she recall that his animation and flirtatious manner were altogether at odds with his claim that he was being no more than dutiful.

This woman's initial presentation of the incident and of her own reaction to it as "superneurotic" reflects what can properly be called a loss of reality. More exactly, it reflects a surrender of her own judgment, including her actual perceptions of reality, in favor of an acceptance of her husband's claim, when rebuked by him.

This, too, might be described as a kind of "double bookkeeping." We have evidence, after all, in the form of her initial distress at her husband's behavior, of the existence of an originally realistic perception and judgment of it. This realistic perception and judgment were then abandoned (though probably not completely, since they were recovered without great difficulty) in the face of her husband's rebuke. In other instances, comparable realistic judgments might never be permitted fully conscious articulation by her, or might never be permitted to form at all. In these cases, a judgment of the reality, if it can be said to exist, is unavailable to her.

In summary, cognition cannot be separated from cognitive attitude, and cognitive attitude, in turn, cannot be separated from the dynamics of the personality as a whole. The anxiety-forestalling modes and restrictive attitudes of neurotic conditions inevitably impede, or limit, or bias the consideration of external reality.

It remains to be seen whether the loss of reality that appears in nonpsychotic pathology bears any relation at all to what we find in psychosis. At this point, however, we are entitled to two conclusions: that the old notion that there is no loss of reality of a general sort in neurotic conditions is false; and that the loss of reality in those conditions, at least, is a direct effect not of a breakdown of characterological defense, but of its workings.

A particular aspect of these conclusions is worth noting further. The loss of reality that I have described in nonpsychotic conditions is not purposeful; it is not motivated by a wish to escape or withdraw from reality. It is, rather, a by-product of the anxiety-forestalling modes and attitudes I have indicated. I make this point because, if comparable processes are in fact at work in psychosis, it suggests a clear alternative to the common view that the psychotic loss of reality is a purposeful "turning away" or "withdrawing" from reality. Sometimes it is assumed that any significant psychological result must be consciously or unconsciously purposeful; for instance, the incomprehensibility of some schizophrenic speech has been thought by some to be motivated by a defensive wish to avoid being understood. However, to borrow the metaphor of Andras Angyal, the rabbit leaves tracks in the snow as it crosses the field in winter, but it does not have a purpose in doing so.

SELF AND OBJECT

We know that a conspicuous symptom of schizophrenia is a weakened or impaired sense of a unified self and, correspondingly, a weakening of the separateness or externality of what is actually external to the self. The latter symptom is often described as a loss of "ego boundaries," following the term coined by Victor Tausk in his paper on the "Influencing Machine" in schizophrenia (Tausk, 1933). Some writers, in fact, consider this loss of boundaries to be the central symptom of schizophrenia (Blatt and Wild, 1976; Freeman et al., 1958).

Of course, the impairment of a sense of a unified self and a distinct external world overlaps greatly with the schizophrenic loss of reality in general, but some of its manifestations are distinctive enough to consider separately. I will illustrate the symptom as it appears in schizophrenia in order to sharpen the discussion. But I mainly want to consider, once again, whether comparable phenomena are to be found in nonpsychotic conditions as well and, if so, whether the processes responsible in the neurotic case can contribute to the understanding of the more radical psychotic case.

The continuous subjective experience of oneself (as distinct from one's *idea* of oneself) seems to be largely implicit. That is, the experience is on the whole not so much a consciousness of oneself as a conscious relationship with, an attitude toward, something external. It is the awareness of self that is contained in a conscious intention or plan regarding an external objective, or even in an attitude of contemplation of something external, an active looking-something-over. The sense of self is in that way contained in what Heinz Werner (1948) calls the *polarity* of self and object. It surely is, also, a constituent of the experience of personal agency and, perhaps, is hardly to be distinguished from that experience.

In daily life that self-object polarity fluctuates a good deal. There are occasions—for instance, while watching a movie—when one allows oneself to become absorbed in an external situation and "loses oneself" in it, which is to say that one loses a clear awareness of its externality. When someone on the screen is hurt, we wince. Or, sometimes, when one becomes absorbed in music, particularly recorded music whose original source is not visible, one loses consciousness of its externality. In habitual or automatic action, also, the self may become relatively transparent; one tends to forget oneself, and at the same time one's consciousness of the external situation tends to be reduced to a reaction to cues and signals. On the other hand, when we are more planful and deliberate, when we become conscious of choices or decisions to be made, of projected possibilities and alternative aims, our sense of self, also, is stronger.

If, as it seems, the experience of the self and of a distinct external world are dependent upon one another in this way, are even aspects of a single experience of a polarity, then the anxiety-forestalling restrictions of subjective life in neurotic conditions must also affect that separateness of the external world at the same time that they weaken the sense of self. If this reasoning is right, in other words, a weakening of both the sense of a unified self and of "ego boundaries" would seem to be a symptom of all psychopathology, neurotic as well as psychotic.

In schizophrenia, as I said, the phenomenon is clear. Tausk, for example, describes a schizophrenic's complaint that everyone knows his thoughts, that his thoughts are not enclosed within his own head but are spread throughout the world, occurring simultaneously in the heads of all persons (Tausk, 1933). The boundaries are, of course, permeable, also, in the inward direction. Tausk's paranoid schizophrenic patient, for instance, complained of the existence of a machine that removed thoughts and feelings by means of mysterious forces, produced motor phenomena in the body, and created various strange sensations. The self was no longer intact, but was invaded and manipulated by external agents.

The experience by schizophrenics of internal body sensations that are alien or not of oneself is not necessarily an explicitly threatening or paranoid one. For example, a patient of Andras Angyal's felt ". . . like other people would stick their head into my head. When I am chewing it seems that another tongue comes and takes the food" (Angyal, 1936, p. 1036).

There are many schizophrenic distortions of the external world that are unaccompanied by such self-distortions and alien internal sensations. But one can see in these, nevertheless, the loss of a polarity, of a distinct sense of both self and object. For instance, commands or reproaches that clearly originate internally are experienced as external: A schizophrenic man, concerned that he is weak and effeminate, reports hearing a strange voice telling him sharply, "Man up!"

In schizophrenia the external world is imbued with striking subjective qualities not only of a more or less ideational kind, a kind that might be products of the imagination, but also of a directly perceptual kind. As Heinz Werner (1948) says, "The properties of things cease to be entirely objective, geometric, and 'out there.'"

> For example, the formerly schizophrenic patient of Marguerite Sechehaye, Renee, writing of the onset of her own schizophrenic episode, describes her teacher's futile effort to reassure her: "But her smile . . . only increased the anxiety and confusion for I saw her teeth, white and even in the gleam of light. Remaining all the while like themselves, soon they monopolized my entire vision as if the whole room were nothing but teeth . . . " (Sechehaye, 1968, p. 22).

Sometimes the schizophrenic's experience focuses on distortions of the external world, as above, sometimes only on internal sensations that reflect the impaired sense of self. But either one generally implies the existence of the other. For example, the following schizophrenic patients report peculiar body sensations:

A schizophrenic man reports that when he passes certain women he feels a strange "buzzing" in the area between his thighs and his abdomen.

A schizophrenic woman describes sexual sensations as "little manny beasties biting me here" (Freeman, et al., 1958).

Where the normal person is conscious of a personal feeling, a sexual interest or some other interest of his own in another person, and is conscious, one might say, of a relationship between himself and that other person, these schizophrenic patients are conscious only of a strange internal sensation and a vague external trigger of that sensation.

Louis Sass argues that an extraordinary introspective awareness is central to schizophrenic experience. Sass points out that the schizophrenic is often peculiarly conscious of body functions and sensations that are normally unnoticed or transparent. He says, ". . . as attention turns inward, the patient begins to notice . . . the saliva in his mouth, the set of his neck . . . (and) the movement of his eyelids begins to feel odd . . . " (Sass, 1992, pp. 227–228).

Sass quotes a schizophrenic patient: ". . . my chest is like a mountain in front of me . . . The arms and legs are apart and away from me and they go on their own . . . I have to stop and find out whether my hand is in my pocket or not" (Sass, 1992, p. 229). The parts and functions of the body are, in other words, no longer constituents or representatives of a unified self, but are alien and under some other control.

Sass proposes that this loss of a sense of a unified self and weakening of the polarity between the self and the external world are symptoms of a relentless self-scrutiny. Such a self-scrutiny, or "hyperreflexivity," he believes, is manifest in the preoccupation with body sensations and mental processes that normally would be unnoticed in the purposeful workings of the body and mind, with the result of the schizophrenic's peculiarly fragmented and alienated body sensations. Sass considers the schizophrenic loss of purposeful, volitional direction, itself, to be a consequence of this relentless introspection, likening the effect to the centipede whose self-consciousness costs it the ability to walk. We will consider the matter of volitional impairment in schizophrenia later, but to anticipate the hyperawareness of body sensations is, in my opinion, together with the weakened sense of a unified self in general, more likely a product of the loss of volitional direction than a cause.

Let us return to our initial questions. Is there evidence in nonpsychotic conditions of an impaired sense of a unified self and a weakening of subject-object polarity that is in any way comparable to what we find in schizo-phrenia? And, if so, what are its dynamics? As to the first question, the an-swer is clear enough: A weakened or fragmented sense of self and a corresponding weakening of subject-object polarity can indeed be shown in every form of neurotic pathology. The dynamic background of these effects is clear as well. They are, again, the inevitable effects of the restrictions of subjective life, including cognition, that constitute the processes of defense. Every agency-diminishing distortion or attenuation of the subjective quality of motivation carries with it a weakened or fragmented sense of self and a weakening of subject-object boundaries. The particular form of that weak-ening of boundaries depends upon the nature of the restrictions of subjec-tive life and the gaps in self-experience involved.

In the obsessive-compulsive case, in fact, the weakening of ego bound-aries is accompanied by very much the sort of introspection and fragmenta-tion of self that Sass describes. These individuals, living under the sway of rules, are very often at a loss as to what they feel or want to do. They do a great deal of soul-searching in an effort to discover what they "should" do. They conduct an inventory of their needs, their wishes, their thoughts. The result of this process, itself a symptom of an anxiety-forestalling, albeit painful, rigidity, is a decidedly fragmented sense of self.

Consider the following example: A young professional man, anxious to marry and have a family, complains that he has never fallen in love. He ex-plains that he evaluates the "appropriateness" of each prospect according to education, family background, physical attractiveness, and such. His aim is to identify the correct woman to marry according to what he considers his "needs": appropriateness to his professional position, suitability for his sex-ual disposition and his general physical appearance, and so forth. The con-clusion is inevitably mixed, an assortment of pros and cons corresponding to those various "needs" or, as one might say, these fragments of self.

This sort of inhibition of the normal motivational and emotional relation-ship with the external figure not only fragments the self but, at the same time, alters the experience of that figure. Where someone else would see a person whom he might like, or fall in love with, or not, this man calculates a rating of appropriateness. Where someone else would be conscious of a per-sonal response to another person, and in that response would experience both himself and that other person, this man is conscious only of his "needs" (compare with the schizophrenic's "buzzing sensation"), on the one hand, and those features of the other (appropriate education, inappropriate height, etc.) that may or may not conform to those needs. This perception of the other one—I think it is reasonable to call it a direct perception rather than an interpretation—reduces her from an independently existing figure to particulars corresponding to certain particulars of his own subjective life. The experience, in other words, reflects a weakness of ego boundaries or of the polarity between the self and the external figure, and that weakness of ego boundaries is a direct result of the subject's anxiety-forestalling rigidity.

This kind of boundary weakening is characteristic of compulsive individuals in quite general ways. Under the sway of rules, they live in a world of things that must be done and things that should not be done. This means that external situations speak to the compulsive person as though with commands. "Opportunity" must be put to advantage whether one welcomes it or not. The unfinished job demands to be finished; it is not simply a job that may be finished or not as one wishes. In such ways, the rules under which the compulsive person lives imbue his circumstances with imperatives at the same time that they obscure his sense of his own wishes.

In other instances, also, obsessively conscientious concerns find or greatly exaggerate qualities in their object that are clearly generated by the concern itself. This is true not only of the exaggerated misfortunes that are generated by obsessive worry but, also, of obsessively scrupulous regrets. The opportunity missed becomes glorious in retrospect; its retrospective value is determined not by its personal appeal but by the scrupulousness of the regret. Much the same process is involved in obsessive indecision. Whichever alternative is about to be foregone must be reexamined against the possibility of error and immediately becomes attractive. In all these instances the polarity of self and external object is weakened as the individual's judgment of the reality is displaced by a rule of scrupulosity.

In other kinds of neurotic character, where the attenuation of the subjective self takes other forms, the loss of subject-object polarity takes other forms as well. When the hysterical person speaks of herself as ruled by her emotions and of her judgments as no more than intuitions, she describes a fragmented sensation of herself. And that fragmented and incomplete sense of herself is a direct effect of the defensive disavowal of active judgment and deliberate action. At the same time, the complement of that hysterical fragmentation of the sense of self is the subjectivity of the hysteric's picture of the world, the subjectivity that romantically idealizes some figures and creates frightful images of others. In other words, the sensation of an emotion-driven self implies less than a clear sense of the external object of that emotion. The normal relationship between one person and another person is reduced to a relationship between an emotion and the creation of that emotion, again a loss of ego boundaries.

A weakened subject-object polarity is evident also in the suggestibility of hysterical people, the ease with which they can be influenced, and in general the weight and authority that other figures carry for them. A hysterical patient sits nervously and momentarily silent in her therapist's office. She then says, as if in apology, "I can't think of anything to say." She adds, "I know you're waiting for me to talk." She plainly experiences the fulfillment of the therapist's expectation as a responsibility of her own. In this way, others' expectations are experienced as requirements, others' opinions have the force of truth. The other's view or expectation, in other words, is not experienced merely as the other's view or expectation, as external, but becomes indistinguishable from the self's.

The externalization of responsibility by the impulsive or psychopathic character illustrates the same point. The psychopath's reactions are too immediate, too spur-of-the-moment to be experienced by him as constituting actual intentions, choices, and expressions of himself. By the same token, those reactions are too quick to allow for contemplation of the external objective. Instead, the objective is experienced only as a trigger, and the action that follows as a reflexive reaction that has been triggered ("She pushed my buttons"). We call the subjective result of this experience an externalization of responsibility, an assignment of responsibility for an action to its external provocation. More exactly, however, the faintness of the sense of self and the self's own intention has the effect of erasing the distinction between an external incentive or provocation, on the one hand, and personal motivation on the other. This loss of polarity, or externalization of responsibility, is also a direct perception. It is not merely a defensive tactic, although the perception may then be defensively elaborated. It is intrinsic to the immediacy of this passive-reactive style. The style itself, however, constitutes a defense.

There hardly is any need to cite further examples. In any neurotic pathology an incompleteness or restriction of the subjective self is bound to result from the defensive reliance on agency-diminishing modes. At the same time, the absence of a firm sense of the self implies less than a clear perception of what is external to the self. In neurotic or nonpsychotic pathology this is, of course, much less obvious than in psychosis and, inasmuch as it is a general and accustomed effect of characteristic style, it lacks the subjective quality of strangeness that is often so much a part of the phenomenon in schizophrenia.

AFFECT

Chronic schizophrenics are often described as apathetic, their affect as "flattened" or "blunted." Observations, such as Arieti's, that at an advanced stage the schizophrenic patient "seems to have completely lost the capacity to feel" are common (Arieti, 1974, p. 375). This "flattening" of affect has usually been understood to reflect the primitivized mental state of these conditions. That view is not contradicted by the appearance in these patients of occasions of abrupt anger and belligerence, or diffuse and apparently uncontrolled excitement.

We shall consider schizophrenic affect further in the next chapter. It is enough to say now that, like the loss of reality and the weakening of ego boundaries, the degradation of the quality of affect has generally been considered a distinguishing symptom of schizophrenia. In psychoanalytic theory the loss of emotional reaction has been regarded as another reflection of the withdrawal of interest in the external world, a turning away.

The fact is, however, that the quality of emotional reaction is impaired in all psychopathology, including nonpsychotic conditions. How could it be otherwise? If the defense processes of neurotic conditions involve general, characterological restrictions and distortions of subjective life, how could the quality of emotional experience remain unaffected? A certain loss of emotional quality is particularly well known in each of the two passive-reactive nonpsychotic conditions that have been discussed, hysterical and psychopathic. The nature of the loss in each of those conditions and a comparison of the two in this respect will be instructive for our understanding of the schizophrenic symptom.

Hysterics, we recall, are known for their extravagant emotionality, but it is an emotionality that is usually described as shallow. Psychopaths are, if anything, emotionally more shallow; they are sometimes sentimental, indeed sometimes given to abrupt mood changes, but more frequently affectively neutral or cold. In the case of either the hysterical or psychopathic condition, the degradation of emotional quality is not hard to understand. In each case, it reflects the characteristic defensive mode. Emotional reactiveness, after all, is not a capability of an independent organ like hearing or seeing. It is an integral aspect of the relationship with the external world, inseparable from the attitudes and modes that shape the nature of that relationship generally. Specifically, the limitations imposed by the passive reactive mode of hysterical character determine the quality of hysterical emotionality and its place in the hysterical person's mental life.

In the normal adult, volitional action has separated distinctly from emotional reaction. A critical relationship between the two remains, of course, but not the original one. Immediate emotional reaction gains weight and durability from other, more stable aims and interests, and in the process is often modified and transformed by them, or it fails to accrue support and vanishes. In this way, if it proves durable, feeling becomes a constituent of personal motivation, an important factor in determining what one wants to do.

The nature of hysterical passive-reactiveness, its immediacy of response, limits such development. The essential process of integration of the immediate reaction with existing aims and interests is foreshortened or short-circuited. The result is an emotionality that is vivid and at the same time ephemeral. This kind of emotional reaction does not feel like a constituent of personal motivation, a personal reason to act and, in that way, a constituent also of the sense of agency; it feels, so to speak, like a wind, sometimes a storm, that strikes the hysterical person, may sweep her into impetuous action or, equally likely, may simply pass. Thus, even highly emotional outbursts may hardly be recognized shortly afterward by the one who experienced them as representing genuine personal feelings. They may be dismissed, for instance, as a product of premenstrual tension, or as an aberrant, "superneurotic" episode, or simply as something "I didn't mean."

Hysterical emotional reactiveness is, also, described as egocentric. That is, it not only tends to be limited to figures or circumstances that are closely related to the individual herself, but it tends to be dominated by the immediate effect of those figures or circumstances on the subject herself. The hysterical woman's description of her teacher as an ogre ("I hate him!") does not express her feelings about him as a distinct figure so much as it expresses his most recent effect upon her. Altogether, the instability, the shallowness, and the egocentricity of hysterical affect are the direct products of the hysterical passive-reactive defensive mode.

In the psychopath, a still more immediate passive-reactiveness has the effect not of increasing emotionality, on the whole, but of diminishing it. But it is an effect in the same direction. The quick translation of interest into action foreshortens, even more than in the hysterical case, the development of a significant, distinctly emotional response, separate from the action itself, to the object of interest. One might say that the psychopath is too quickly absorbed in accomplishing his immediate aim to permit an emotional contemplation of the object of that aim or the effects of accomplishing it.

> A psychopathic patient, asked by his therapist how he would respond if they met outside when the therapist possessed something that he wanted, answers: "I'd take it. If need be, I'd take you out, but you know, it's nothing personal. I kind of like you" (Wishnie, 1977, p. 136).

The emotional indifference of the psychopath, as compared with his interest in an immediate gain, represents a further step in the shallowness and egocentricity of affective reaction. To put the matter more sharply, it represents a further step in the shallowness and egocentricity of the individual's emotional relationship with the external world.

The general characterological distinction I suggested earlier between hysterical and psychopathic character holds for the dimension of affective quality. It is the distinction between a defensive hypertrophy of a passive-reactive mode of comparatively less immediacy and one of comparatively greater immediacy; between an adult, predominantly female, defensive adaptation of an early mode of activity and an adult, probably predominantly male, defensive adaptation of a mode whose origins are probably somewhat earlier. In both cases the quality of affect suffers as a consequence of the passive-reactive mode. The degree of that degradation of affect is related to the immediacy of that reactiveness.

It is useful here to recall once again that emotional response is a developmental achievment. The separation of emotional response, feeling, from action comes with development. The objectification of the world, the development of a firm sense of the self and of an increasing capacity for intentional and planful action—all this further diminishes the early reflexive immediacy and totality of reaction and brings further differentiation and refinement to the quality of emotionality. We can perhaps derive a general principle concerning the quality of adult emotionality from this developmental picture, without implying any simple correspondence. When the capacity for reflective and planful action is weakened or defensively curtailed in favor of a passive or rigid mode of immediate reactiveness, the quality of emotionality will be proportionally reduced. This principle seems to hold in the case of the shallow emotionality of the hysteric and in the case of the still more shallow emotional neutrality of the psychopath. We shall see later if it is useful for the understanding of the chronic schizophrenic.

LOSS OF VOLITIONAL DIRECTION AND THE SENSE OF AGENCY

In the previous sections of this chapter, I have wanted to show that a loss of reality, a weakening of ego boundaries and a degradation of affective quality, all usually considered defining symptoms of schizophrenia, are in fact present in nonpsychotic conditions as well. I wished to show, also, that in nonpsychotic conditions, at least, those formal symptoms can be understood not as a failure of defense, but rather as products of defense, specifically, effects of the defensive retreat from the experience of agency to prevolitional, rigid, or passive-reactive modes of diminished agency. Up to this point in our comparative study, the familiar formal symptoms of schizophrenia could be taken for granted, requiring only some specification in some instances; I have emphasized the demonstration of comparable symptoms in their neurotic forms. What follows, however, will have a somewhat different focus.

Here, I want to consider the radical schizophrenic loss of volition, its quality and certain of its effects, and at the same time to clarify the relation of that loss of volition in schizophrenia to the neurotic avoidance and loss of agency. The aim here, therefore, remains the comparative study of the two kinds of conditions to determine if the dynamics of one can aid in understanding the other.

In earlier work (Shapiro, 1981), I have argued that a loss or weakening of the experience of self-direction (synonymous in my use with agency) and a corresponding attenuation of the actual processes of volitional action can be seen in *all* forms of psychopathology. On the whole, however, those symptoms—actually, the subjective and objective descriptions of the same symptom—have been identified in different ways in neurotic conditions and in schizophrenia. In other words, both the schizophrenic loss of volition and the neurotic avoidance of agency are well known, but they are well known separately.

The neurotic avoidance of agency, at least in connection with particular symptomatic actions, is more than familiar to psychoanalysis. The severing of consciousness of intention from unconsciously motivated action is, after all, fundamental to psychoanalytic understanding of symptomatic behavior. It has long been understood (Fenichel, 1941) that psychoanalytic treatment aims precisely to transform the initially passive and estranged experience of the symptom into an awareness of its active motivation. In more recent years, as I indicated earlier, the loss or disclaiming of consciousness of agency has been recognized as a more general and in fact central aspect of neurotic conditions (Schafer, 1976), its therapeutic restoration equivalent to cure (Kaiser, 1955/1965).

If the neurotic loss of agency has been well recognized in psychoanalysis, the objective impairment of volition in schizophrenia is no less so in general psychiatry. If anything, as I will describe shortly, it is more widely recognized because it is more obvious clinically. Yet nowhere in psychoanalysis or psychiatry, to my knowledge, is the relationship between the neurotic's diminished experience of agency and the schizophrenic impairment of volition made explicit and clear. The elements of a significant relation are known independently, but they are described in two different languages, and where that relation should be apparent, there is a gap.

There is a reason for that gap. It reflects the difference in the nature of clinical interest in schizophrenia, on the one hand, and neurotic conditions, on the other. Interest in schizophrenia has focused on the general form of behavior and mentation, whereas interest in neurotic conditions has been largely limited to the content of subjective experience and its dynamics. The relationship between the impairment of volition and the avoidance of the experience of agency, however, becomes apparent only with the recognition of the dynamic significance of the general form of activity.

The defensive motivation to avoid consciousness of agency or personal intention cannot in itself account for its avoidance; agency cannot be effectively disclaimed at will, apart from particular behaviors that might be rationalized in one way or another. The distortion of subjective experience must be founded on some objective psychological process. The general avoidance or attenuation of the experience of agency is accomplished in nonpsychotic conditions by a general attenuation or distortion of the processes of volitional action. It is, for example, the psychopath's spur-of-the-moment action and its foreshortening of the normal volitional processes, the processes of decision, that makes it possible for him to avoid clear consciousness of his own intentions and to experience instead some external agent as responsible for his action. Thus we are led to the possibility that the impairment of volitional direction in schizophrenia may also constitute an anxiety-forestalling reversion—in this case a radical one—to prevolitional modes.

Clinical observers of schizophrenics regularly note a severe impairment of volition. Arieti, particularly, declares that schizophrenia is above all a pathology of volition. The phenomenon is noted, also, by Goldstein (1944), Angyal (1937), and others (including Bleuler, Kraepelin, and Jung), and described variously as an impairment of volition, will or intentionality, or as a condition of extreme passivity, or as stimulus-boundedness or concrete reactiveness. These observations for the most part do not refer merely to passivity in the behavioral sense of inactivity or submissiveness. They refer to an inability, or unwillingness (on this point there is some difference, although the predominant view is of an inability) to initiate a course of action, to make a considered choice, or even to concentrate, to focus or shift attention at will.

Essentially, these clinical observations have been confirmed in, for the most part, more recent controlled and experimental studies. The impairment in schizophrenia of selective attention or attentional "filtering" (See, for example, Chapman and Chapman, 1973; Frith, 1979); of ability to shift attention at will or sustain attention in a given direction (Venables, 1987); of initiation of action (Frith and Done, 1988); of "central control" (Shakow, 1977); and of "executive" functioning as in cognitive flexibility or forward planning (Morice and Delahunty, 1996) have been confirmed in controlled studies, although experimental workers mainly assume a direct neurophysiological cause for such impairments and do not relate the loss of particular cognitive function to a more general loss of volition.

There is no doubt, however, that schizophrenia presents a picture of an impairment, or inhibition, or abandonment—at any rate, a profound loss— of active, volitional self-direction, including particularly cognitive self-direction. In clinical observation, at least, this frequently takes the form of an extreme kind of passivity. Hence the less formal but perhaps more descriptive psychiatric term "schizophrenic surrender."

In a general way this passivity is familiar to anyone who has witnessed the peculiar inertia of chronic schizophrenic patients on the wards or the grounds of psychiatric hospitals, particularly in the days before the wide use of psychoactive medications. But a loss of volitional self-direction can take many forms, and it has been observed and reported in a great variety of circumstances and in a variety of schizophrenic conditions.

Perhaps the most vivid behavioral example is the well-known, although now apparently rare, catatonic condition of "waxy flexibility." These patients initiate no movement, remaining more or less immobile in whatever position they are placed. It is significant that catatonic immobility is sometimes interrupted by episodes of "catatonic excitement," described as frenzied (Nunberg, 1948/1961) and aimless action, "movement salad, the motor equivalent of word-salad" (Arieti, 1974, p. 81). This kind of activity, though in dramatic contrast to immobility, is by no means inconsistent with a failure or abandonment of volitional direction; it only reflects an alternative expression of such a failure or abandonment.

> But apart from such extremes, observations such as the following, reported by Angyal, are not rare: "When (the patient) arrives at the door, a new problem arises for him, namely, to cross the threshold. For a long period he steps forward, then backward, until finally he enters the room . . . every detail of the desired action must be separately demanded of him. For example, it is not sufficient to tell him that he may leave the room. He must be told to stand up, to walk, to open the door, etc." (Angyal, 1937, pp. 1048–1049).

We will consider the dynamics of that kind of volitional failure in the next chapter, but it is important to point out here that apart from its behavioral manifestations, a great deal of schizophrenic delusional content directly reflects the subjective experience of a radical loss of volitional self-direction.

> For example, a schizophrenic patient, referring to her own utterances, says, "It's not people speaking, it's a tape" (Rosenbaum and Sonne, 1986).

In the case of paranoid schizophrenics, of course, ideas and experiences of losing volitional control to external agencies or struggling against such loss figure regularly in delusional preoccupations. Ideas of being controlled by rays, hypnotically controlled, or mentally influenced by machines controlled by others are common.

The paranoid schizophrenic Schreber repeatedly complains of having "to bellow like a wild animal because of miracles enacted on me" (1955, p. 227). Schreber speaks, also, of the "closing of [his] eyes" due to "the power of the rays," mysterious control of his fingers while playing the piano, being forced by the rays to "perform movements" (p. 40), and so forth.

It is the loss of volitional direction of thought and attention in schizophrenia, made clear both by well-established clinical observation and, more recently, controlled and experimental studies that is surely the most serious kind of volitional failure and, among the pathologies considered here, the most distinctively schizophrenic. It is this kind of failure that is described, for example, by Goldstein as "concreteness" and characterized by thinking that is "directed by the immediate claims made by one particular aspect of the object or situation" (Goldstein, 1944, p.18); or by Bleuler as an "impairment of active attention," as opposed to "passive attention," which is retained (Rapaport, 1951, p. 638). And it is this kind of volitional failure that is described by contemporary researchers as attentional deficit or an impairment of cognitive flexibility and executive cognitive functioning or an inability to maintain a set or change the set quickly when necessary.

All these authors, though they do not use the term, describe a passive-reactiveness of the most profound sort. It is a passivity, often in the form of passive distractibility, which is manifest in various sorts of schizophrenic thought disorder. It is evident, for example, in the so-called tangential thinking of schizophrenics, in which associative connections lead the train of thought away from its original point. It is probably responsible, also, for the capture of attention by language fragments, word or phrase sounds and other immediately evocative stimuli, with the result, sometimes, of erratic shifts of level of thought and consequent confusion.

Indeed, it was proposed, although later rejected, by a prominent investigator, C. D. Frith, that the failure of consciousness to select and maintain a direction while inhibiting alternatives (the defective filtering hypothesis) may be responsible not only for such symptoms of thought disorder, but also for schizophrenic auditory hallucinations. Frith suggested that these are constructed around preconsciously perceived extraneous sounds that a more actively directed attention would exclude from consciousness (Frith, 1979). He later rejected his "defective filter" conception in favor of one of defective initiation and monitoring of action (Frith and Done, 1988). Both conceptions, however, include the notion of a loss of directed activity, whether perceptual or monitoring.

The finding that the formal dimensions of schizophrenic symptoms that we have considered are intrinsic also to nonpsychotic pathology lends support to the hypothesis that similar dynamics are at work in both. That hypothesis, that schizophrenic symptoms are the product not of a collapse of an existing defense structure but of its radical extension, has a clarity and a subjective logic that its alternative lacks. It posits a familiar process, that increased anxiety will trigger an increased reliance on anxiety-dispelling modes that are already employed. We expect, for example, that a rigid person will be driven by further anxiety to greater rigidity. This does not mean that the resulting symptoms of such a defensive intensification will necessarily be simple exaggerations of the previous symptoms. Sometimes they will be; the obsessive person under conditions of stress may become more obsessive. But sometimes, in some people, the increased reliance on prevolitional modes, particularly if the reversion to those modes is profound, may produce a qualitative transformation of symptoms. That is, such a defense reaction may produce quite different symptoms that are, however, still understandable as products of those previously employed modes. The development of a paranoid rigidity from an obsessional rigidity is an example of this. The development of schizophrenia may be another.

It may be worth noting once again that this psychological hypothesis is in no way inconsistent with the assumption of a biological predisposition. On the contrary, if it should turn out that such a predisposition includes, for example, some subclinical deficit of focal attention, a defensive employment of that deficit in the form of a reaction of the sort we are considering would only be that much easier to imagine.

CHAPTER 8

Schizophrenia

In the previous chapter four dimensions of the individual's relationship with the external world were considered. Those dimensions, to be sure, overlap considerably; they are aspects of a unitary relationship and one cannot imagine damage to any one of them that would leave the others unaffected. But it is the dimension of volitional direction and its subjective sense of the self's agency that is central to our interest here. That is so because it is the process of volitional self-direction and the consciousness of one's own agency that seem directly to evoke anxiety and—speaking for the time being only of nonpsychotic pathology—it is the anxiety-forestalling surrender of volition and agency that, in turn, affect the individual's relationship with the external world as a whole. The rest, the loss of reality, the weakening of boundaries, the degradation of affective quality, all seem to be by-products of that curtailment, that process of defense.

We have so far considered these effects and processes primarily as they appear in nonpsychotic pathology. The question now is whether the same defensive processes and their effects hold for schizophrenia as well. To put the question more sharply, we want to know whether schizophrenic symptoms, like neurotic symptoms, can be considered products of the curtailment—in this case, however, the radical, perhaps even disabling curtailment—of volitional direction in favor of rigid or passive-reactive prevolitional modes. There is substantial evidence in the psychiatric literature in support of this supposition. It is mainly clinical evidence, but it is consistent among a large number of observers. I have already referred to some of that evidence, and it will be considered more closely in the first section of this chapter. Following that, I will propose an understanding of the transition to schizophrenia from certain neurotic conditions as it appears from this standpoint.

THE LOSS OF VOLITIONAL THOUGHT AND ATTENTION

There is no serious question about the essential phenomenon, the schizophrenic impairment of volitional direction of thought processes, specifically of attention. On that point the verdict is unanimous; experimentalists and clinical investigators agree. One might add that impairment of concentration, as opposed to passive attention, is a standard sign of schizophrenic thought disorder in diagnostic psychological testing. The large questions remain, however, as to whether the loss of volitional direction of thought and attention is secondary to other, perhaps more fundamental, cognitive processes or is the primary deficiency in schizophrenia from which its other symptoms derive; and, if the latter, whether it can be understood as a defensive reaction or, on the contrary, is a directly biological deficiency. The influential work of Andrew McGhie and James Chapman is particulary interesting with regard to both these questions.

McGhie and Chapman (1961), on the basis of interviews and subjective reports from schizophrenic patients, consider the failure of volitional self-direction, including volitional direction of thought, to be central to the symptoms of schizophrenia. However, they regard that volitional failure as an expression of a still more fundamental cognitive impairment, an impairment of the "selective-inhibitory mechanism of attention." The conception is an early version of the experimentalists' defective filtering hypothesis. McGhie and Chapman assign that cognitive impairment (as the experimentalists do), though rather tentatively, directly to biochemical deficiencies. McGhie and Chapman's work and its experimental continuation is critical to our argument, and we will consider it in more detail, but a word concerning their conclusion of a direct biochemical cause is in order now. The issue concerns the general relationship between cognition, on the one hand, and psychodynamics on the other.

McGhie and Chapman, although themselves psychoanalytical, reject any understanding of schizophrenia based solely on traditional dynamic considerations of particular conflicts. That is, they reject the idea that schizophrenic symptoms are "defensive activities purposefully related to unconscious conflicts over interpersonal difficulties" (p. 103). They insist instead that the basic problem has to do with the "mental apparatus" of the schizophrenic, by which they presumably mean the relevant biochemistry. The conviction that the *form* of schizophrenic symptoms cannot be understood in terms of family dynamics would find little disagreement today (nor would it have, probably, from Freud). The assumption, which is generally followed by the experimentalists in this field, that such dysfunction can only be assigned directly to biochemistry is another matter.

McGhie and Chapman's conception of psychological dynamics is the traditional psychoanalytic one; it is limited to the family dynamics of particular childhood conflicts. There is probably *no psychopathology*, neither psychotic nor neurotic, whose essential *form* can be understood in terms of those dynamics. This is, in fact, an old problem, one with which psychoanalysis is quite familiar; it is none other than the problem of the so-called choice of neurosis, and it has proved over the years to be essentially intractable in terms of the traditional dynamics. The form of neurotic symptoms and, if we are correct, the form of schizophrenic symptoms as well, require for their understanding a more inclusive picture of dynamics, a picture that recognizes the *forms* of thinking and modes of activity as central to the mind's regulatory system. That regulatory system, the individual character organization, one might say, constitutes a "mental apparatus" in the *psychological* sense.* It may indeed be affected by variations of individual biology as well as by personal history, but the existence of a psychological mental apparatus that includes the individual forms of cognition makes the assumption that cognitive deficiencies must have direct biological causes unnecessary.

In fact, as we have seen, cognitive processes are invariably involved in the dynamics of character, and the symptoms of psychopathology invariably include some impairment of cognitive function. It is exactly that relation between psychological dynamics and cognition, and the evidence in neurotic conditions of the effects of dynamics on cognition, that point us toward the hypothesis we are now considering, namely that the symptoms of schizophrenia, though not themselves defensively purposeful, are products of a radical surrender of volitional direction of thought that is defensive in origin.

---

*David Rapaport often spoke, in lectures and conversation, of mental "apparatuses" in this psychological sense.

Let us return to the important cognitive evidence offered by McGhie and Chapman (1961). Patient after patient in their investigation reports an inability to direct or focus attention at will. "Everything seems to grip my attention" (p. 104), says one patient. Another patient says, "I am distracted and forget what I was saying" (p. 104). Yet another says simply, "I can't concentrate" (p. 104).

The failure of volitional direction of attention seems to be experienced by these patients primarily in the form of continual distraction. They are passively susceptible to "everything at once." The authors conclude that these patients can no longer direct their attention "at will"; their attention is now "being increasingly determined . . . by concrete changes in the environment" (McGhie and Chapman 1961, p. 105).

Much the same experience is described by other schizophrenic or formerly schizophrenic patients. The former schizophrenic Renee, for example, speaking of the onset of her psychosis, exemplifies this capture of attention "by concrete changes in the environment":

> "During class, in the quiet of the work period, I heard the street noises—a trolley passing, people talking, a horse neighing, a horn sounding, each detached, immovable, separated from its source, without meaning . . . On the platform, the teacher, too, talking, gesticulating . . . " (Sechehaye, 1968, p. 24).

Similar distractibility has often been found in experimental studies of schizophrenics and, in fact, has been found to be a stable trait, present even in those who were nonpsychotic at the time of testing (Harve et al., 1990).

The inability to direct attention at will or to sustain it in a given direction, with the resulting capture of attention by extraneous cues, is responsible, McGhie and Chapman also suggest, for the peculiarities of schizophrenic language use. The schizophrenic is captured by the sounds of words or word-fragments and loses his point. Thus one of their patients says that he "may suddenly get bogged down at a word . . . It's as if I am being hypnotized by it . . . seeing the word . . . in a different way . . . It's not so much that I absorb it, it's more like it's absorbing me" (McGhie and Chapman, 1961, p. 109).

Very similar observations of an attention remarkably lacking in purposeful direction or focus, particularly in connection with perception, are reported by Matussek (1987, pp. 92–94). Speaking of an essentially static environment, Matussek states that the schizophrenic is "held captive" by an isolated object. This "rigidity of perception" is manifest in a continuous staring in which the patient loses himself ("spellbound") in contemplation of a particular object. In this contemplation, the object becomes separated from its context. The schizophrenic patient reports that he saw only "fragments, a few people, a dairy, a dreary house. To be quite correct (I cannot say that I did see all that because), these objects seemed altered from the usual. They did not stand together . . . and I saw them as meaningless details" (p. 92).

The prolonged and peculiar staring that has been noted in schizophrenics by others, and is discussed particularly by Louis Sass (1992, p. 47), appears to be a passive and unfocussed fixation in which the subject loses himself in the object. That is to say, he loses a sense of his separateness from, and sense of looking at, the object, while the object loses its usual identity and remains only as a form and a visual sensation.

Matussek mentions that this experience can sometimes be achieved by normal subjects with prolonged gazing, although such sustained gazing is, he says, very difficult for normal people. (I myself have found it possible to produce such experiences with relatively little effort, but not to sustain them.) Matussek mentions that the experience of losing oneself, being "held captive," in the contemplation of an object or perhaps a fragment of an object may occur in normal subjects in a state of fatigue. The experience is also familiar to him from his experiments with mescaline. Numerous others have, of course, reported similar experiences under the influence of mescaline or drugs with comparable effects.

The author William S. Burroughs, for example, writes that during his drug addiction, he "could look at the end of [his] shoe for eight hours" (Burroughs, 1984). Baudelaire described his experience of hashish intoxication somewhat more poetically: ". . . personality vanishes . . . the perception of things in the outer world makes one forget one's own existence and soon draws one into it . . . The eye fixes itself on a tree . . . In the tree one's passions come to life . . . and soon one is the tree itself" (quoted by Werner, 1968, p. 82).

Also commonly reported by subjects under the influence of mescaline or lysergic acid is the experience of being captivated by strong sensory effects such as the vividness of colors. Something of the same experience is reported in accounts of early schizophrenia:

A patient of McGhie and Chapman's says, "Colors seem to be brighter now, almost as if they are luminous" (1961, p. 105). Another patient reported that "noises all seem to be louder" (p. 105).

Renee, in the memoir cited earlier, recalls that when she entered the principal's office at the beginning of her psychosis, it was "illuminated by a dreadful electric light." She speaks, also, of the "yellow vastness [of a wheat field], dazzling in the sun" and, as she anxiously approached her teacher, seeing "her teeth, white and even in the gleam of light . . . soon they monopolized my entire vision as if the whole room were nothing but teeth under a remorseless light" (Sechehaye, p. 22).

Cutting and Dunne (1989, p. 229) found that some schizophrenics they studied report similar experiences: "Lots of things looked psychedelic. They shone."

These unusual perceptual experiences would seem to lend support to the defective filter hypothesis referred to earlier. But the defective filter itself easily may be seen as a result of the failure, or absence, of an active, purposeful focus. It is such a focus that normally organizes visual sensations and particular forms into familiar realities. Normally, in other words, these fragments and sensations are subordinated to the active interest in looking-at-something. They are instrumental to this interest and they lose the power to compel attention to their independent existence when attention is purposefully directed to the recognition of things and situations.

It does seem to be possible for anyone, by prolonged gazing, to exhaust the normal attitude of *looking*, and to experience at least briefly a more passive attitude of only *seeing*, an attitude in which attention settles on fragments and on commanding sensations. Painters are trained in such an attitude. Japanese painters are said to achieve this visual experience sometimes by looking at a landscape upside down, seeing it through their legs and, in this way, disrupting the usual context and objectness of things. But it seems that when the normal volitional direction of attention falters, and with it the actively purposeful looking-at-things, fragmented and isolated forms and sensations emerge without effort.

Many of the well-known peculiarities in schizophrenic thinking and speech seem very much of a piece with these perceptual effects. Normal, more or less purposeful thought and the normally communicative or expository aims of speech are not sustained in schizophrenia, and the weakness of such active purpose permits distractions of thought and language very much like the distractions of attention and perception cited above. Hence "loose associations" or "tangential" thinking, in which a train of thought is derailed by logically irrelevant associations, sometimes based on normally unnoticed alliterative syllabic similarities or word sounds ("clang" associations).

An example is cited by Bleuler: "A hebephrenic wants to sign her name to a letter as usual: 'B. Graf.' She writes 'Gra' and then a word beginning with 'gr' comes to her mind; she corrects the 'a' to an 'o' and adds a double 's,' making 'Gross,' and then repeats this twice . . . The patient thus loses himself in insignificant side associations . . . " (Rapaport, 1951, p. 591).

Bleuler, who considered loose associations to be a central symptom of schizophrenia, did in fact consider the appearance of such associations to be the result of a lack of "goal-presentation, the most important determinant directing associations" (Rapaport, 1951, p. 586). David Rapaport, commenting on these remarks of Bleuler's, adds that "From the point of view of psychoanalysis [also], goal-presentation is the crucial characteristic of the secondary [realistic thought] process" (Rapaport, 1951, p. 586).

I myself have found that an experience of word sounds and fragments comparable to the perceptual effects described earlier can be achieved by a passive repetition of words without a communicative purpose. The result of such a wandering attention seems to be exactly what we call loose or tangential thinking. The schizophrenic hyperawareness of body sensations is probably a similar effect. An absence of purposeful movement and purposeful attention results in increased awareness of normally unnoticed physical sensations.

There is another kind of evidence, evidence, so to speak, from the opposite direction, that the failure, or abandonment, of volitional direction and the organizing effects of purpose are responsible for the loosening of both perceptual and language processes. It seems that the general level of function of schizophrenics, not only in the early stages of the condition but, also, in the later, more chronic stages, are markedly, if temporarily, improved when purpose is imposed on them by external circumstance. Numerous anecdotes are familiar to those who have worked in mental hospitals, especially in the days before psychoactive medications, of patients responding to real emergencies or simple demands of circumstance with unexpectedly normal judgment and behavior. Sechehaye's patient Renee once again illustrates the point when, speaking of her earliest, terrifying experiences of unreality, she says, "What saved me that day was activity. It was the hour to go for prayer, and . . . I had to get in line . . . to do something definite and customary helped a great deal" (Sechehaye, 1968, p. 22).

Perhaps the point is supported in a similar way by evidence that essentially immobile catatonic patients can be engaged in activity, although only temporarily, when ball playing (Straus and Griffith, 1955), dance therapy, or movement therapy (Johnson, 1984) is more or less imposed on them. Indeed, one investigator (Johnson, 1984) suggests that playing ball in such a situation may engage the catatonic patient's responsiveness precisely because it "allows (him) to avoid responsibility . . . for willed actions . . . " (p. 306). In other words, when purpose is imposed, as it can be if personal agency is circumvented, normal activity can be elicited.

Yet another, quite striking, observation by Thomas Freeman points in the same direction. Speaking of catatonic schizophrenics, he remarks: "All the patients were similar in that coherent, fluent, and logical speech appeared when they were angry or under the pressure of a need [such as hunger]. . . . Most often, this 'improved' cognition appeared when the patient was in a withdrawn, unresponsive state in which blocking affected both speech and volitional movement. After the anger there was always a reversion to the earlier state" (Freeman, 1969, p. 93). The momentary emergence of spontaneous purpose, possible under these conditions without self-consciousness, organizes thought and speech.

LOSS OF REALITY AND SUBJECT-OBJECT POLARITY

It is impossible to imagine any volitional impairment, especially one as radical as the schizophrenic's, without comparable damage to the cognitive relationship with the external world. The replacement of an active and intentional mode of *looking-things-over or listening-to-something* by a helplessly passive mode of only *seeing* or *hearing* what seizes attention brings with it a loss of the contextually meaningful objectness and externality of things. In the extreme case, to stare or hear passively and without focus, to be held captive by the stimulus in this way, is to lose oneself in it, to become "absorbed" in it, as McGhie's patient said. The reports by McGhie and Chapman's patients of the fragmented perceptual effects cited above regularly include some such mention of losing oneself in the sensation or losing a sense of separation from its source.

One schizophrenic patient says, "Everything seems to go through me" (p. 104). Another reports getting "mixed up about where sounds are coming from" (p. 105). Reporting such effects, one patient says that he feels like he is "going into a coma" (p. 109); another speaks of "a sort of trance" (p. 109). The experience, it is interesting to note, resembles the induction of hypnotic trance, often aided by a passive staring at an object and sometimes by the instruction to avoid deliberate thought.

At the same time, this passivity-induced loss of subject-object polarity makes possible the animation of the object by the subject's own subjective experience. When the external object is no longer experienced as a distinct thing in a coherent setting, it no longer resists such distortions and transformations. Consider once more in this connection Renee's report of approaching her teacher with extreme anxiety. She sees "her teeth, white and even in the gleam of light . . . soon they monopolized my entire vision as if the whole room were nothing but teeth under a remorseless light."

This is not an experience of a distinct, external figure, a figure looked at or considered, as one might normally do. It is the experience of a helplessly immobilized attention that has been captured by a visual fragment out of its real context. Having lost its own reality, that fragment can more easily be imbued by Renee's anxiety with a sinister quality. Exactly the same effect can be seen in the acutely paranoid, defensively alert person. His attention is seized by a word or two from the radio, perhaps even a fragment of a word. The external context that gives realistic meaning to those words is lost to him, and they therefore can easily be endowed with a threatening significance.

In the previous chapter I described the neurotic loss of reality. There is, for instance, the subjectively colored world of the hysteric looking at the Rorschach inkblot: "A big bat! Spooky!" It is an impressionistic perception that follows from the inhibition of more deliberate and critical judgment. As I pointed out, something comparable can easily be seen in the obsessive person. He learns of an opportunity, or what he thinks should be regarded as an opportunity. He does not, he cannot, actually evaluate this opportunity, look it over, decide whether it is in fact interesting to him. His conscientious rules forbid such an evaluation. Instead, he tells himself the opportunity may never come again; its value is thereby exaggerated and it becomes mandatory. In each of these cases, the hysteric and the obsessive, the polarity between the subject and the external reality is compromised, and the external object or situation is imbued with qualities—"spooky" in the one case, irreplaceable value in the other—that are generated in the subjective life of the neurotic person. This loss of subject-object polarity is a direct effect of the defensive cognitive restrictions of the neurotic character.

In schizophrenia, where the surrender of volition and the cognitive limitations that follow from that surrender are far greater, and the boundaries of self and external object are far weaker, much less is endowed with much more. Bits and pieces of the external world taken from their context reveal themselves as embodiments of large anxieties and ideas:

An early schizophrenic young woman hears the quiet, innocuous murmurs of people passing her on the street as a sinister hissing aimed at her, "Psst! Psst!"

The schizophrenic Schreber, at the beginning of his illness, becomes aware at night of a "crackling noise," which he recognizes as "undoubted divine miracles" (Schreber, 1955, p. 64).

Another schizophrenic patient recalls the impression, while gazing at a slowly swinging light cord, that it was the wall behind it that was moving, and that this indicated the end of the world (Matussek, 1952, p. 93).

These experiences are not the products of interpretation, of ideas of metaphorical or symbolic significance. The delusional quality, as Matussek in particular emphasizes, is "experienced directly as inherent in the object (p. 98)." In other words, the subjective quality of the schizophrenic experience is exactly comparable to the way in which the bat looks "spooky" to the hysteric or the opportunity feels obligatory to the obsessive. To understand the delusional quality of the experience otherwise, as symbolic or metaphorical, in the usual sense of an image that is employed to represent a concept, would fail to recognize sufficiently the loss of an objective world.

If this analysis of the schizophrenic loss of reality is correct, that loss of reality is not itself a defense reaction. It is not, in other words, a defensively motivated turning-away from reality or the external world. It is, rather, like the neurotic loss of reality, a by-product of a defense reaction, of a reflexive, anxiety-forestalling surrender, or profound loss, of volitional direction.

SCHIZOPHRENIC AFFECT

McGhie and Chapman believe that the changes in schizophrenic affect can be counted as secondary effects of the primary, biochemically produced, cognitive disturbance. That is, they regard affective changes as reactions to the experience of a loss of volitional cognitive control and the accompanying loss of the individual's sense of his own "subjectivity." Essentially, the loss of affect, from this standpoint, follows from the loss of a focused object of affect.

A general dependence of the form of affectivity on the status of cognition does, in fact, seem reasonable, even inevitable. For Piaget, cognition provides the structure for affective energy (Piaget, 1981). He saw a series of stages of affective development, for example the early appearance of stable individual attachments and the later development of abstract values, as corresponding to cognitive development from birth through adolescence. It seems to me, however, that the conception of a simple dependence of the form of affectivity upon cognition is not exactly one-sided, but is too limited. The form of cognition and the quality of affect are, together, aspects of the individual's relationship with the external world. They both reflect the general nature of that relationship and the general modes of reactiveness and activity that characterize that relationship. Those modes, rather than cognition alone, provide the structure for affective reaction.

In the previous chapter, I suggested that there is a direct relation between the reversion to prevolitional modes and the degradation of affective quality. I offered as illustration two instances of passive-reactiveness: hysterical character and psychopathic character. The first of these is characterized as emotionally "shallow"; the second more immediately reactive, as not merely shallow emotionally but emotionally "neutral." I propose now that we can extrapolate that relation to the schizophrenic's more profound passivity and correspondingly "flattened" affect.

In chronic schizophrenia, that passivity is so great, the mind's purposiveness and direction are so frail, and the mind, in that sense, so helplessly erratic, that an emotional relationship of any stability, or an emotional reaction integrated to any degree with stable aims or interests, or even an emotional contemplation of an object, is difficult to imagine. The processes of normal emotionality are short-circuited in a far more radical way than in the case of the hysteric or the psychopath. This level of passive-reactiveness, in fact, would seem to account not only for a loss of emotionality but, also, for the appearance of rudimentary and alienated sexual and aggressive reactions, in place of genuinely emotional ones.

Kurt Goldstein, discussing the effects on lower mental functions of an impairment of higher functions due to cortical lesions, makes a comparable point regarding sexual attitude: "The attitude toward the erotic sphere has been modified in the same way as the total attitude towards the world. Just as the latter becomes more stimulus-bound, less independent and less ego-determined, so also does the former become more passive, less discriminating and more disconnected from the ego . . . the difference could be best expressed . . . as a degradation from erotics (love sentiment) . . . to bare sexuality which lacks the more spiritual and more subtle bodily qualities" (Goldstein, 1939, 1963, p. 488).

TRANSITION TO SCHIZOPHRENIA

If it is true, as it seems, that the defensive retreat from agency and volitional direction that we see in neurotic conditions is at work also in schizophrenia to more profound effect, the question of what distinguishes one type of pathology from the other becomes all the more conspicuous. For there is no doubt of a symptomatic discontinuity between the two, often fairly abrupt in the development of the psychosis, and nothing that we have considered so far explains it.

In neurotic conditions, of course, the impairment of the relationship with external reality is limited. This implies more than merely the degree of impairment. The neurotic character has developed slowly and has been influenced in its development by the demands and opportunities of external realities. The pathology has developed, so to speak, mindful of adaptive requirements as well as internal ones. The flighty, but socially engaging hysteric; the rigid, but productive worker; even the impulsive and psychopathic man of action are all familiar and, in their respective ways, adaptive types. This has no serious parallel in schizophrenia. (The development of anxiety-forestalling neurotic styles that are also adaptive suggests, in fact, that where adaptive requirements are different, as in other times and places, neurotic symptoms might be expected to have somewhat different forms, whereas this would not be expected for schizophrenia.) The existence of such adaptive successes for neurotic styles, in obvious contrast to schizophrenia, however, has a further significance than only as a measure of comparative mental health: It means that the neurotic relationship with external reality, however compromised, is yet sufficiently intact to provide external nourishment for volitional direction.

Volitional direction, self-direction according to conscious aims, cannot function, cannot even be imagined, in the absence of external objectives.* Intentionality and volition develop in infancy together with the consciousness of such objectives—the infant must recognize the rattle as an interesting object in order to reach for it—and they remain dependent upon the existence of external objectives. So far, we have considered the relation between volitional direction and the experience of external reality only in one direction: the weakening of the experience of external reality that follows from the restriction or loss of volition. But when we consider schizophrenia, an effect in

---

*See the discussion in Chapter 2 of Shapiro, 1981.

the other direction must be considered, also: the effect on volitional direction of a loss of clear external objectives.

We have experimental data on such effects, at least under extreme conditions. Experimental arrangements that deprive normal subjects of ordinary sensory contact with the external world (through the use of soundproof cubicles, translucent goggles, etc.) shortly produce symptoms likened by the experimenters to those produced by mescal or lysergic acid intoxication (Bexton et al., 1954; Heron, 1957). The symptoms are also markedly schizophrenic-like. They include hallucinations, strange body sensations ("something seemed to be sucking my mind out through my eyes" [Heron, p. 54]), and affect disturbances (both irritability and spells of easy amusement). The symptoms include, also, a loss of volitional control of thought and attention much like that experienced by the schizophrenic patients quoted here. In general, these subjects reported that it took too much effort, or they were simply unable, to concentrate. They "abandoned attempts at organized thinking" (Bexton et al.) and "let the mind drift" (Heron). The experimenters describe these effects as a "deterioration in the capacity to think systematically and productively." One experimental subject, reporting sensory experiences like those we have discussed, said, "My mind just became full of sounds and colors and I could not control it" (Heron, p. 54).

I am proposing that the discontinuity between the neurotic and the psychotic state may be a result of the reciprocal effects of a loss of volitional direction and the weakening of subject-object polarity that is attendant upon it. Some loss of external reality, of subject-object polarity, is present in all psychopathology. In certain individuals, however, that loss of a clear and stable sense of external reality, although a by-product of the defensive retreat from volitional experience, may in turn assume proportions that deprive the individual of the external objects that volitional direction requires. I take this to be the point in incipient schizophrenia at which anxious, even terrifying, feelings of strangeness and unreality appear. A further and accelerated movement to an extreme, that is, schizophrenic, rigidity or surrender of volition may then occur. As Harry Stack Sullivan describes the typical onset of schizophrenia, "The disturbance in reality appraisal which has been slow in the prodromal stages is now very swift" (Sullivan, 1962, p. 113).

A process of this sort may be reflected, for example, in those cases of gradually increasing obsessional preoccupation that then fairly abruptly become frankly schizophrenic. The young man who has, with increasing urgency, been collecting enormous amounts of data on all the colleges and universities in America, with the supposed aim of plotting his further education and career, becomes at a certain point unsure of his purpose, confused, extremely anxious, and aware that something is wrong with him; he then rapidly develops strange and grandiose ideas. What had been a neurotic, that is, obsessional, rigidity, under considerable pressure, loses reality to the point of great anxiety and confusion (Sullivan describes this experience, typical of incipient schizophrenia, as one of "perplexity" (Sullivan, 1962, p. 115) a feeling that things are "wrong" (p. 114), and symptoms of a much more extreme rigidity appear. What was a defensive retreat from volitional experience becomes, with sufficient weakening of the relationship with external reality, an outright volitional disability, one that extends to the direction of attention and thought.

This reciprocal process seems quite compatible with the assumption of a biological predisposition or a process "involving two variables" suggested by Philip S. Holzman on the basis of both clinical psychological and genetic data. Holzman suggests that an existing subclinical pathology, represented in a specific type of thought disorder (looseness, etc.) and present only in moderate degree in, for example, unaffected relatives of schizophrenic patients, may then become exacerbated to the point of schizophrenia (Holzman, 1995). I propose that such an exacerbation may be produced in certain individuals by a defensive retreat from volitional experience.

RIGIDITY IN PARANOID AND
CATATONIC SCHIZOPHRENIA

I have suggested that, in a limited sense, schizophrenia, like nonpsychotic symptoms, can be considered "in character." I mean by this that the symptoms of schizophrenia, for all their emergent differences, are further products of the defensive reactions characteristic of the prepsychotic personality. Now I want to make this formulation somewhat more specific and show that the radical schizophrenic loss of volition and its symptomatic consequences can be understood as further products of the specific prevolitional modes characteristic of the particular prepsychotic condition.

I have chosen the paranoid and catatonic forms of schizophrenia as examples because we have some fairly clear information on the typical prepsychotic setting of each of these conditions. There is considerable evidence that the typical prepsychotic character of each of these types of schizophrenia is marked by some form of obsessive-compulsive rigidity. My aim, then, is to show that each of these schizophrenic conditions can be understood as a radical, presumably anxiety-driven, exaggeration of a rigidity of that kind. It is true that we cannot describe with any exactness the pertinent distinctions within this coarse category, neither the distinctions between the typical prepsychotic settings for each, nor even the more general distinction between the kind of rigidity that may lead to psychosis and the much more common kind that will not. The processes I shall describe, therefore, can have no predictive value; they will be too general and imprecise for that. But even such a general description of these processes may offer at least some retrospective understanding of the development of schizophrenia.

It will be recalled that the relation of obsessive-compulsive to paranoid styles derives above all from the fact that any rigid mode of self-direction involves conflict and resistance to influence on two fronts, internal and external. In the more stable case of the obsessive-compulsive the struggle is essentially internal, though not entirely; he is also stubborn. But wherever both internal and external fronts must be guarded, any instability on the internal front is inevitably translated into a vulnerability on the external front. One has only to imagine a less stable transformation of the obsessive-compulsive, less assured that he is what he "should" be, therefore more self-conscious and to that degree less absorbed in productive work, to arrive at a picture no longer merely of stubbornness and rigid purpose, but of an intensified rigidity and a defensive sensitivity. In other words, one arrives at a picture of a paranoid condition.

The cognitive bias and the consequent loss of reality that is always an aspect of this kind of sensitivity and defensiveness increases, becomes more rigid, as that defensiveness intensifies and becomes stiffer. The element in the external world that satisfies defensive anticipation is, increasingly, seized from its context; increasingly, that element, out of whatever surrounds it, seems to *command* notice. The more rigid the bias, in other words, the more immediate is the recognition of the confirming element, and with that immediacy of recognition, subject-object polarity diminishes. As the guarded patient enters the therapist's office, he sees on the shelf, at some distance, a book with the word "hypnosis" in its title. In that instant, so to speak, a threatening hypnotist is created out of the patient's guardedness. As the confirming element becomes easier to discover, less and less in reality is required to satisfy expectations that are more and more fixed and more and more urgent. All this, I think, is well established. I have conjectured further that when such a loss of external reality progresses to a certain point, a new anxiety and disorientation overtake the existing dynamics and accelerate that process. When a paranoid defensive mobilization and its cognitive bias reach an extreme of rigidity, elements of reality that confirm defensive expectations are discerned so easily and so immediately that they are no longer experienced as discoveries; they strike the eye. They present themselves constantly and unavoidably.

> For example, an acutely paranoid man, terrified of the conspiracy against him, reports that threatening messages now "jump out" at him from billboards and the newspapers.

The immediacy with which these "messages" are recognized and the rigidity of bias that that immediacy reflects marks a virtually complete loss of boundary or polarity between the self and the external reality. That immediacy, the triggering of a fixed and programmed idea as if by a signal, reveals with special clarity the essentially passive-reactive nature of a cognition that is this rigidly biased. The short-circuiting of volitional direction of thought and attention in this way is schizophrenic.

It is well known, however, that in paranoid schizophrenia, in contrast to the more plainly passive types of schizophrenia, a certain orderliness of thinking is typically retained (Blatt and Wild, 1976). That orderliness reflects, I assume, that this kind of rigidity, dominated as it is by particular ideas of great intensity, still retains in its fixed pursuit of those ideas a certain independence of external and internal distraction. This to some extent distinguishes it from more profoundly and more generally passive forms of schizophrenia.

Severely obsessive conditions are recognized as a setting, not only for paranoid schizophrenia but for catatonic schizophrenia as well. This is yet another reminder not only of the coarseness of our diagnostic categories, but of the limitations of our understanding. At any rate, granting this serious limitation, the association of obsessive traits and attitudes of a certain type with catatonic schizophrenia is well known clinically. It should be noted that those traits and attitudes are not only commonly identified in the history of catatonic patients; they are often conspicuous when the schizophrenic process is well underway.

For example, in a review by David Read Johnson of eight case reports—all he was able to find—of the psychotherapeutic treatment of catatonics, obsessive traits or compulsive symptoms are conspicuous in each. Obsessive perfectionism in particular is noted frequently (Johnson, 1984). Thus a patient of Otto Will's "berated himself for not being 'perfect enough'" (p. 302); Herman Nunberg's patient had attempted to "'perfect himself' through a program of physical exercise" (p. 300); Robert Knight describes his catatonic patient as "perfectionistic, obsessional" (p. 300). Apart from that particular trait, a patient of Silvano Arieti's is described as "overwhelmed with obsessive doubts, indecision" (p. 301); and Johnson, the review's author, describes his own patient as "almost immobilized when faced with a decision" (p. 304).

But it is not merely the fact that these symptoms are present in catatonics that is of interest. That, in itself, might be interpreted in various ways, perhaps as no more than residual features of obsessive-compulsive defenses that have failed and are therefore quite separate from the subsequent catatonic condition. Actually, the relation, as it is revealed in the reports of formerly catatonic patients, is much more intrinsic than that. The experience of the so-called catatonic stupor, in fact, seems in important respects to be a direct continuation and intensification of certain kinds of obsessive experience.

The catatonic immobilization seems specifically to reflect a radically exaggerated obsessional hesitancy, indecision, and precautionary concern. The nature of that radical exaggeration can be defined more clearly; it consists of a scrupulosity that, in its rigidity, is well beyond that of the obsessional neurotic. It is this rigid scrupulosity that is expressed in the perfectionism noted above. In catatonic immobilization, no action, that is, no intentional action, can pass its inspection.

Consider, for instance, Silvano Arieti's description of a patient actually "in the process of developing a catatonic attack" (Arieti, 1974, p. 318): "More and more he realized that it was difficult for him to act. He did not know what to do . . . where to look, where to turn. *Any motion* that he was inclined to make appeared to him as an insurmountable problem, because he did not know whether he should make it or not . . . The *overwhelming fear of doing the wrong thing* . . . seemed to possess him . . . Therefore he preferred to be motionless" (my emphasis).

Arieti summarizes his observations quite clearly: "The patient who is to become catatonic is generally a person given to . . . overpowering anxiety, especially anxiety connected with the carrying out of some action . . . The anxiety will then be . . . generalized to every action, to every movement determined by the will [i.e., every volitional movement]" (p. 155).

A catatonic patient described by Andras Angyal illustrates the nature of this anxiety more specifically: "Every little movement he made assumed an almost cosmic significance. He had the feeling that even lifting a finger or taking a step would have incalculable important consequences . . . he would stand motionless in the same spot for hours . . . Sometimes . . . he 'stealthily' stretched his neck, but he felt very guilty about it as if he had done something wrong" (Angyal, 1950, p. 155).

Another catatonic patient, a fifteen-year-old girl, illustrates much the same attitude, in this instance in connection with a more specific concern. She is terrified of causing damage to (hallucinated) flies on the floor and will not permit either herself or anyone else any movement in the room: ". . . she stands in the middle of (the room), staring keenly at the floor and being careful not to move from the spot. Her cheeks are puffed up with saliva, which she obviously cannot let herself either swallow or spit . . . " (Tahka, 1993, pp. 290–91).

One might easily observe that in the scrupulousness of their precautions, these patients can hardly be distinguished from obsessive individuals, except of course for the enormous exaggeration and unreality of their concerns. But even this distinction is far from sharp. For the scrupulousness of neurotically obsessive precautionary concerns and worries also produce unrealistic exaggerations. As we have seen, obsessive people, in their anxious concern with self-control, often construct alarming pictures of their "impulses." If they were to relax that self-control, they tell us, they might rape an innocent child, drive off a bridge, become promiscuous, abandon all responsibility, or worse. These specters are products not of ordinary judgment, but of a rigidly biased and relentless search for dangerous or improper thoughts. The more exacting and scrupulous that search, the more extreme its bias will be, and the more horrific its "discoveries."

The dynamics of the obsessive are relevant, also, to Arieti's observation, quoted earlier, that the catatonic schizophrenic's anxious inhibition of a particular action generalizes to all volitional action. Generalization of that sort is not the result merely of a cognitive tendency to generalize. Obsessive anxieties also commonly generalize, although not so extensively; it is intrinsic to their dynamics to do so. It is precisely the rigid scrupulousness, the relentlessness, of obsessive precautionary concerns with personal error or culpability or misfortune, the fact that such concerns cannot be laid to rest, that no stone can be left unturned, no remaining possibility overlooked, that drives the obsessive person's concern from one worry to the next and to more and more remote possibilities.

Obsessive individuals, of course, also experience on certain occasions a general inhibition of action, a kind of immobilization or "paralysis"—that is the common subjective report—that in extreme cases may actually resemble a catatonic state. Such an immobilization is sometimes the outcome of particularly severe instances of one of the most common of obsessive symptoms, indecision, again an expression of a rigid scrupulosity that finds fault, or worse, in every inclination to action.

One such severely obsessive man, at the time a patient in an open psychiatric hospital, was frequently observed standing motionless for extended periods on nearby street corners. He was actually sometimes mistakenly assumed to be catatonic by hospital personnel who happened by at such times. But he was not schizophrenic, only agonizing about which way he "should" go and unable to choose.

We have considered the similarities between the obsessive and the catatonic, but we must also consider the critical distinctions. The case just cited is helpful in several ways in drawing the distinction between a severely obsessive inhibition of volitional action and a genuinely catatonic immobilization. Of course, one can say that the catatonic case is simply more extreme. Obviously the precautionary specters conjured by the catatonic are even more remote from reality than the often far-fetched concerns of the obsessive, and the inhibition of volitional action is therefore more complete. Despite the tendency of obsessive anxieties to generalize, indecision and its inhibition of action are usually limited to particular occasions when consciousness of personal choice is unavoidable and the accompanying self-conscious experience of agency is therefore acute. This was the situation in the case just cited. (It has been noted by one observer with puzzlement [Rapoport, 1989] that obsessive patients may have particular difficulty at the point of crossing thresholds. The problem of course is not one of thresholds, but one of the decisions.) Action that is routine or otherwise dictated by rules or circumstances, however, is typically untroubled for obsessive people. For the catatonic, on the other hand, self-consciousness and inhibition has extended to all action. This difference reflects a more fundamental one: The catatonic is considerably more extreme than the obsessive specifically in the *rigidity* of his scrupulousness. That more extreme rigidity, we will see, has distinctive symptomatic consequences. But first the nature of that rigidity needs further explanation.

The internal authority of rules in the rigid person's self-direction can take various forms, and can take those forms in various degrees. For instance, rules, while experienced as rules or "should's," can still be comparatively close to actual personal convictions and values—a generous person may think that he *should* be more generous. Then, too, many rule-based attitudes leave wide latitude for personal interpretation. This is the case for the typical compulsive attitude that demands constant productiveness but generally does not specify its nature or quality. On the other hand, internal rules also can be exceedingly exacting or perfectionistic in their requirements, and the more exacting and perfectionistic those rules are, the finer their net and the fewer the actions that escape their prohibitions. If we say that the catatonic is more extreme in his rigid scrupulousness than the obsessive, it is in the specific sense that his scrupulousness is far more exacting. The most obvious reflection of this exacting scrupulousness is the extensiveness or generality of its prohibitions. As Arieti says of his catatonic patient: Even in the period prior to the actual catatonic state, "Every action . . . became loaded with a sense of responsibility. Every willed movement came to be seen . . . as a moral issue" (Arieti, 1974, p. 161).

But the effects of such an exacting scrupulosity go beyond a mere extension of its domain. It is not only that wider areas of behavior and thought come under examination. More important, as behavior and thought become subject to an examination that is increasingly exacting in its identification of dangerous or iniquitous thoughts or actions, or the possibility of horrific consequences of such thoughts or actions, that examination becomes increasingly biased and leads inevitably to distortion and exaggeration of the possibilities and the consequences of trangression. This, in turn, has a further consequence. The closer and more exacting the examination and the more minute and technical its evidence, the more immediate (as in the paranoid case) its identification of those possibilities. In sum, the polarity of subject and world is progressively lost and in place of ordinary judgment, another world of iniquitous and dangerous action and horrific consequences is constructed.

Thus, Silvano Arieti describes the symptoms his patient Sally experienced prior to lapsing into a catatonic stupor: "She had the impression that small pieces or corpuscles were falling down on her body or from her body. She preferred not to move because she was afraid that her movements would cause small pieces to fall . . . it kept her in mortal fear of any movement . . .

She used to ask relatives to help her do the searching for her, to reassure her that no bodies were falling" (Arieti, 1974, p. 148).

Once again, I offer the conjecture that such a loss of polarity between the subject and external reality is at some point itself disorienting with the result that fresh anxiety accelerates an already increasing rigidity. In any case, however, a loss of polarity of this degree brings us to a further distinction between the paralysis of obsessive indecision and that of the catatonic.

For the one who is only obsessively conscientious, hesitation to act, indecision, even periods of apparent paralysis or frank inhibition of action are still experienced as being in some degree active, as deliberate (despite the subjective report of "paralysis"). The restraint of action, often justified by rationalizations, is not separated from judgment by such distance as to eliminate all sense of agency. In the catatonic case, this seems finally to be the case. The experience of inhibition ultimately becomes a subjectively passive one. Another catatonic patient of Arieti's, for example, experienced himself "solidifying." He "was like a statue of stone" (Arieti, 1974). This kind of experience is yet another ramification not merely of rule-directed action, or rather, prohibition of action, but of rules that are remarkably rigid and exacting.

As these rules become more exacting, they also become more alien. Something of this tendency in more moderate degree is observable, even symptomatically conspicuous, in obsessive-compulsive conditions. To the extent that obsessive conscientiousness becomes more technical and fastidious, the typically nagging consciousness of "should's" tends to take on more obviously symptomatic forms; "should's" and "should not's" become "must's" and "must not's." In other words, as the rules of rigid self-direction become more legalistic, more exclusively occupied with minute infractions, and therefore more remote from personal judgment, the behavior that follows from those rules feels progressively more remote from personal choice. In this way, an obsessive conscientiousness is replaced in some measure by the more alien experience of compulsion.

To put the point more generally and, also, more simply, a greater rigidity implies a further diminishing of the sense of agency. In the catatonic case, this development is far advanced. When the restraint of action is dictated by rules whose prohibitions are so rigid, so exacting, and so devoid of any participation by personal judgment or conviction, the result is a passive and alienated experience of the effects of those prohibitions. The experience is no longer one of deliberate restraint, but of surrender and paralysis.

In some catatonic cases the nature of this surrender has yet a further symptomatic consequence. A total surrender of volitional direction of action may have, after all, two alternative expressions: The state of catatonic immobilization is one; the other is uncontrolled activity, activity without conscious restraint or direction. Thus, in some cases the so-called catatonic stupor may be interrupted at times by abrupt, impulsive acts or by the extremely agitated and uncontrolled state of catatonic excitement.

SCHIZOID CONDITIONS

Although the development of paranoid and catatonic schizophrenia from certain obsessive modes seems comparatively clear, there is no doubt of other routes to schizophrenia. The most obvious is its emergence from a setting of schizoid character. As compared with obsessive and other neurotic conditions, however, there is unfortunately not only a certain vagueness about the nature and dynamics of schizoid character but even a good deal of variation in the common descriptions of its symptoms. Nevertheless, the existence of this type of character and certain of its fundamental features have been recognized for a long time.

Thus, Helene Deutsch, in a famous paper originally published in the 1930s, describes the schizoid (or "as if") person as characterized by "a remarkable passivity of the ego" (Deutsch, 1942, p. 316). This description is subsequently elaborated on in the psychiatric literature in several directions. For example, Harry Guntrip describes these individuals as apathetic, lacking in energy, with a "laissez faire attitude" (1969, p. 19) and often leading "empty, innocuous, docile and inconspicuous lives." Very frequently they are described as drifters or as "drifting through life." Sometimes they are also described as being occasionally impulsive or even somewhat psychopathic. It is not only in the behavioral sense that they are considered to be remarkably passive, therefore, but very much in the sense that I have used the term passive-reactive, lacking or avoiding fully volitional, purposeful self-direction.

The description of schizoid individuals as drifters is particularly interesting not only because it gives a vivid picture of the quality of their passivity, but also because it suggests something of their relation to the psychopath. Drifting through life might be said to describe a more passive form of the erratic life that is typically psychopathic. The psychopath, in his opportunism, is quick to react to the situation of immediate personal interest and exploit it. He is passive in the immediacy with which his interest can be captured by the opportunity (or the provocation) that presents itself; hence his life-course is erratic. But he is active in his quick pursuit of that opportunity. Drifting implies an even greater lack of active self-direction. The drifter, also, is easily diverted this way and that, but, one thinks, as much or more by the pressure of circumstance as by opportunity. Perhaps one could say that the drifter passively waits for what comes up, while the psychopath is more actively on the lookout for what comes up.

A lack or impoverishment of emotion is also considered a fundamental characteristic of schizoid individuals. They are usually described as "callous" or "unfeeling," although sometimes giving the appearance of feelings that they do not have (hence Deutsch's depiction of them as "as if" personalities). In their apparent lack of emotionality also, therefore, they resemble the psychopath. If one remembers the capacity for sentimentality often noted in the psychopath but seemingly absent in the schizoid personality, however, one realizes that in this respect, too, the passivity of the schizoid, the absence of a genuinely emotional interest in the other, is more profound than that of the psychopath. Yet it is clearly less so than that of the chronic schizophrenic.

Although it is the general lack of emotion, or the "emptiness," as it is sometimes called, of schizoid individuals that has in particular identified their condition as related to schizophrenia, cognitive similarities have also been noted. Thus Guntrip (1969) speaks of a "derealization of the outer world" and an experience of "things being out of focus or unreal." Both the emotional and the cognitive impairments have generally been regarded, much like those of schizophrenia, as reflections of a withdrawal or turning-away from the external world and especially from human relationships. But just as with schizophrenia, one may question whether the impaired relationship with the external world is actually a motivated turning-away, as is supposed, or is, rather, an effect of other processes. For, once again, the defensive retreat from volition to a deeply passive reactiveness of diminished agency, with its further psychological consequences, seems to hold also for the schizoid condition and seems to make its symptoms understandable. That view makes comprehensible as well that a further deepening of passivity may result in the development of schizophrenia.

"DOUBLE BOOKKEEPING"?

I would like to return now to the interesting suggestion by Louis Sass that the schizophrenic's delusions actually exist together with a capacity for realistic thought, in a system he characterizes as "double bookkeeping." If this proposal is valid, it affects our conception of schizophrenia in quite a central way. For "double bookkeeping" clearly implies that schizophrenia does not involve damage or deterioration of the ordinary cognitive system. It implies, instead, that the ordinary cognitive system continues to exist, only being in some sense suspended and partially displaced in consciousness by an alternative ideational system.

Sass reminds us that "the patient who insists her coffee is poisoned with sperm still drinks it without concern, the Virgin Mary or the Queen of England continues, without protest . . . to perform the same menial tasks as other patients" (Sass, 1992, p. 274). It is not hard to find comparable examples: A schizophrenic outpatient who claims to spend his days doing his "work" as president of the United States never fails to keep his psychotherapy appointments at the low-cost clinic. We do, in fact, have numerous reports from recovered schizophrenics that seem exactly to confirm the existence of such a double point of view.

> For example, a formerly catatonic patient, delusional, hallucinatory, and incontinent during his hospitalization, says afterward that throughout the entire period he had "in the back of [his] mind the feeling that everything would turn out all right in the end" (Angyal, 1950, p. 157).

> Many reports are more explicit. Sechehaye's patient Renee says, when describing her terrifying experiences at the early stage of her schizophrenia, "Nonetheless, I did not believe the world would be destroyed as I believed in real facts" (Sechehaye, 1968, p. 27).

It is not only in retrospective accounts that such detachment is reported. Consider the following exchange between the schizophrenic patient cited above, who often referred to his presidential work, and his psychotherapist.*

PATIENT: "I ought to tell you . . . I think you're a lot of different people in disguise."

---

*Reported to me by Dr. Meir Ekstein.

THERAPIST: "You say you *think* that I am."

PATIENT: "Well, of course I don't *believe* that you are! I see you right in front of me!"

Evidence such as this of a realistic point of view alongside a delusional one is not rare. But neither is it invariably present. The delusional patients who carry out hospital chores like ordinary citizens are often passively following direction and cannot be said on that account to be making realistic judgments. For that matter, delusional patients are frequently able to reconcile their circumstances with their delusions, insisting, for instance, that they are in the hospital incognito or conducting themselves with the discretion required by their special mission. A schizophrenic patient of Angyal's, for example, "believed that his confinement in the hospital was just another test that he had to pass" (Angyal, 1950, p. 154). Finally, there are certainly schizophrenics who do not show any signs of "double bookkeeping" at all, who do not perform hospital chores like ordinary citizens, and may, in fact, flee the city in terror of their imagined persecutors. And some schizophrenics, even in these days of psychoactive medication, remain generally incoherent. Regarding "double bookkeeping," therefore, we have evidence of at least two quite different sorts. That, perhaps, should not be a surprise; we know, after all, that there is a great variety of schizophrenic states.

The "double bookkeeping" conception contains two propositions. The first is that the delusion does not reflect a damaged cognitive process, but an alternative ideational process and an alternative relationship with the external world. This, perhaps, would be a trivial assertion if it were not supplemented by the second proposition. The second proposition holds that such an alternative ideational process is actually compatible with the existence more or less at the same time of an ordinary judgment and a realistic relationship with the external world, at least in regard to practical matters.

The first proposition holds that the delusion is not *believed* in the same sense as an ordinary judgment. It is not a false belief or a faulty judgment, as some psychologists have suggested; it not a belief at all. As Sass puts it, the delusion is not regarded with belief, but with a suspension of disbelief. One could put the point in somewhat more general terms: The delusion reflects a *suspension of ordinary judgment* altogether in regard to its subject matter. The notion gains interest, and perhaps clarity, because, as I mentioned earlier, it exactly characterizes the case of obsessive worry or regret.

When we hear that the obsessive individual thinks that the door he has just locked might still be unlocked and should be checked once more, we understand without question that his idea does not reflect a damaged or faulty cognitive process but an alternative process. Ordinary judgment has been suspended, probably temporarily and in any case only in regard to a particular subject matter. We naturally assume that this person will be capable of realistic judgment in other matters. In this case, in fact, we are able to describe the alternative, that is, obsessive, ideational process and its relationship to reality quite clearly. We know that the obsessive worry ("maybe it's still unlocked") reflects the precautionary requirements of a rigidly conscientious attitude. The requirements of that attitude prohibit a normal consideration of external reality. They prohibit the employment of, or at least the reliance on, the normal cognitive process.

Although this "double bookkeeping" is particularly clear in the obsessive case, it is actually characteristic of all neurotic conditions. Its basis is the existence of internal conflict and a characterological defense system. It is the existence of that conflict and defense system that gives the speech and behavior of neurotic people in general a certain artificiality or ungenuineness,* as in the exaggerated fearfulness of the hysteric ("It's spooky!") or the forced spontaneity of the hypomanic. The defensive retreat to prevolitional modes of rigidity and passive-reactiveness is restrictive and it is not free of tension; those defensive modes do not represent the totality of the person. But the neurotic person himself will not generally be aware of the schism between what he presents to others and to himself and what he actually feels and thinks, between what he thinks and feels and what *he thinks* he thinks and feels. In that sense, the processes we are considering are unlike real double bookkeeping; they are not processes of deception, but of self-deception.

It is true, of course, that the obsessive person says, in regard to his worry or regret, "I think . . ." or "I might have . . ." whereas the delusional individual—say, the delusional paranoid individual—expresses certainty, often emphatically so. But the certainty of the delusion is a special kind of certainty. It is not like the ordinary experience of looking (or thinking) things over and arriving at a judgment. It is a more immediate experience and a more pas-

---

*Such an artificiality was considered by Hellmuth Kaiser to be the "universal symptom" of all neurotic conditions (Fierman, 1965).

sive one. It is a discovery that reveals itself abruptly, often by a single hint or clue, never genuinely puzzling, equivocal, or disappointing:

> The delusional patient of Angyal's, remembering an incident of a few nights earlier, "knew at once with certainty" that he had received orders for a special FBI assignment. On another occasion, when asked for directions by a stranger on the street, *suddenly he knew* that their meeting was not accidental" (Angyal, 1950, p. 153).

A cognitive process that results in this special kind of certainty follows from the character dynamics I have described. The paranoid mobilization against external threat is at this point extremely urgent, the defensive attitude is extremely rigid, and the bias, the prohibition of a proportioned consideration of reality, is extreme. A circumstantial element sufficient to precipitate the idea that is already waiting is bound to present itself forcefully and without conscious effort. In a word, the schizophrenic delusion is a *revelation*, and its certainty is the special certainty of a revelation. Perhaps only a hallucination, for which no external cue is necessary, would reflect an even greater loss of polarity and would present itself with an even greater immediacy. (The same patient of Angyal's, shortly after the events just cited, did in fact experience auditory hallucinations that he described as "a revelation.") All this is to say not only that the schizophrenic's belief in his delusion is a different kind of belief from an ordinary judgment, and the product of quite a different cognitive process from ordinary judgment. It says, also, that the delusional belief is based precisely on a prohibition of ordinary judgment.

The fact that the delusion is not a faulty judgment or a false belief but an experience of revelation can account for the phenomenon that Sass describes as "double bookkeeping." For quite apart from the matter of realistic validity, if the delusion is not a judgment, we cannot expect it to have the coherence, the relative stability, and the motivational significance that are typical of judgments. Delusions may sometimes lead to further actions in the external world, as judgments typically do, but they by no means do so regularly. They may be sufficient ends in themselves. Like obsessional concerns, they are after all much more expressions of the individual's relationship with himself than with the external world.

Whether or to what extent or in what circumstances ordinary judgment and the ordinary cognitive relationship with the external world is permitted will be determined by the momentary requirements of internal dynamics. When, for example, the sensation of threat is acute, the defensive mobilization will intensify, and ordinary judgment may be eclipsed by delusion. When the sensation of threat is diminished, that mobilization will in some measure relax, interest in the delusion will diminish, attention will extend beyond the threatening clue, and ordinary judgment will have its say. We see that kind of fluctuation of cognitive style in neurotic conditions and we see it in psychosis as well, particularly in early, acute psychotic reactions.

> Thus an acutely paranoid patient, who begins a therapeutic hour with an agitated and terrified description of the conspiracy against him and the threatening messages directed at him through the radio, ends the hour in quiet conversation, with a rueful, though still uncertain, smile about his own irrational concerns. Several hours later he is once more terrified of the conspiracy.

Shall we regard this kind of fluctuation as between two distinct cognitive systems or modes rather than simply as one system of varying quality? Both theory and observation seem to weigh in favor of two different systems, each with its own impetus. The one system is adaptive, its function to consider reality,s whereas the other is not adaptive, its function purely to forestall anxiety. It is possible, in chronic psychosis, for ordinary judgment to be more or less completely, perhaps even permanently, excluded by internal requirements and prohibitions. But it is sometimes also possible, though far more easily in neurotic conditions than psychotic ones, to perceive the results of two distinct cognitive attitudes at the same time, one more conscious than the other, one expressed in what is said, perhaps with emphatic conviction or alarm, the other still noticeable in the speaker's glance or voice.

References

Abraham, Karl (1924/1953). Manic-depressive states and the pre-genital levels of the libido. In *Selected Papers of Karl Abraham* New York: Basic Books.

Angyal, Andras (1936). The experience of the body-self in schizophrenia. *Archives of Neurology and Psychxiatry* 35: 1029–1053.

Angyal, Andras (1937). Disturbances of activity in a case of schizophrenia. *Archives of Neurology and Psychiatry* 38: 1047–1054.

Angyal, Andras (1950). The psychodynamic process of illness and recovery in a case of catatonic schizophrenia. *Psychiatry* 13:149–165.

Arieti, Silvano (1974). *Interpretation of Schizophrenia. 2d ed.* New York: Basic Books.

Austin, J. L. (1962). *How to Do Things with Words.* Cambridge: Harvard University Press.

Bateson, Gregory (Ed.) (1961). *Perceval's Narrative: A Patient's Account of His Psychosis.* Stanford: Stanford University Press.

Bexton, W. H., W. Heron, and T. H. Scott (1954). Effects of decreased variation in the sensory environment. *Canadian Psychololgy* 8:2.

Blatt, Sidney J., and Cynthia M. Wild (1976). *Schizophrenia: A Developmental Analysis.* New York: Academic Press.

Bleuler, Eugen (1951). The basic symptoms of schizophrenia. In David Rapaport, *Organization and Pathology of Thought.* New York: Columbia University Press, 581–649.

Burroughs, William (1984). *Naked Lunch.* New York: Grove Press.

Cacioppo, John T., and Gary G. Berntson (1992). Social psychological contributions to the decade of the brain: Doctrine of multilevel analysis. *American Psychologist* 47: (8), 1019–1028.

Chapman, Loren J. and Jean P. Chapman (1973). Disordered thought and schizophrenia. New York: Prentice-Hall.

Cloninger, C. Robert (1978). The link between hysteria and sociopathy: An integrative model of pathogenesis based on clinical, genetic and neurophysiological observations. In *Psychiatric Diagnosis: Exploration of Biological Predictors*, Hagop S. Akiskal and William L. Webb (Eds.). New York: Spectrum.

Custance, John (1952). *Wisdom, Madness and Folly: The Philosophy of a Lunatic.* New York: Pellegrini and Cudahy.

Cutting, John, and Francis Dunne (1989). Subjective experience of schizophrenia. *Schizophrenia Bulletin*, 15 (2): 217–231.

Deutsch, Helene (1942). Some forms of emotional disturbance and their relationship to schizophrenia. *Psychoanalytic Quarterly* 11:301–322.

Eagle, Morris (1987). *Recent Developments in Psychoanalysis.* Cambridge: Harvard University Press.

Erikson, Erik (1950). *Childhood and Society.* New York: Norton.

Evdokas, Andreas (1997). *An Attempt to Induce a Hypomanic-like State in Normal Subjects Through Rapid Production.* Ann Arbor, MI: VMI.

Fenichel, Otto (1941). *Problems of psychoanalytic technique.* Psychoanalytic Quarterly Press, 1945.

Fenichel, Otto (1948). *The Psychoanalytic Theory of Neurosis.* New York: Norton.

Fierman, Louis (Ed.) (1965). *Effective Psychotherapy: The Contribution of Hellmuth Kaiser.* New York: Free Press.

Freeman, Thomas, John L. Cameron, and Andrew McGhie (1958). *Chronic Schizophrenia.* New York: International Universities Press.

Freeman, Thomas (1969). *Psychopathology of the Psychoses.* New York: International Universities Press.

Freeman, Thomas (1976). *Childhood Psychopathology and Adult Psychoses.* New York: International Universities Press.

Freeman, Thomas (1981). Quoting Maurits Katan in the pre-psychotic phase and its reconstruction in schizophrenic and paranoiac psychoses. *International Journal of Psycho-Analysis* 62: 447–53.

Freud, Anna (1937). *The Ego and the Mechanisms of Defense,* London: Hogarth Press and the Institute of Psychoanalysis.

Freud, Sigmund (1911). Psychoanalytic notes upon an autobiographical account of a case of paranoia. Standard edition 12:3. London: Hogarth Press, 1958.

Freud, Sigmund (1913). The disposition to obsessional neurosis. Standard edition, 12 London: Hogarth Press, 1958.

Freud, Sigmund (1922). *Group Psychology and the Analysis of the Ego.* Standard Edition 18: 69. London: Hogarth Press, 1958.

Freud, Sigmund (1928). *The Ego and the Id.* London: Hogarth Press.

Freud, Sigmund (1926/1959). *Inhibition, Symptoms, and Anxiety,* Standard Edition 20:77. London: Hogarth Press.

Freud, Sigmund (1937). Analysis terminable and interminable. Standard Edition 23: 238. London: Hogarth Press.

Frith, C. D. (1979). Consciousness, information processing and schizophrenia. *British Journal of Psychiatry* 134: 225–235.

Frith, C. D. (1987). The positive and negative symptoms of schizophrenia reflect impairments in the perception and initiation of action. *Psychological Medicine* 17: 631–648.

Frith, C. D., and D. J. Done (1988). Towards a neuropsychology of schizophrenia. *British Journal of Psychiatry* 153: 437–443.

Goldstein, Kurt (1939). *The Organism.* Boston: Beacon, 1963.

Goldstein, Kurt, and Martin Scheerer (1941). Abstract and concrete behavior, An experimental study with special tests. In *Psychological Monographs* 53:2.

Goldstein, Kurt (1944). Methodological approach to the study of schizophrenic thought disorder. In *Language and Thought in Schizophrenia*, J. S. Kasanin (Ed.). New York: Norton.

Graves, Alonzo (1942). *The Eclipse of a Mind*. New York: Medical Journal Press.

Green, Maurice R. (Ed.) (1964). *Interpersonal Analysis: The Selected Papers of Clara M. Thompson*. New York: Basic Books.

Guntrip, Harry (1969). *Schizoid Phenomena, Object Relations and the Self*. New York: International Universities Press.

Harve, Philip D., Nancy Docherty, Mark R. Serper, and Myrna Rasmussen (1990). Cognitive deficits and thought disorder: II An 8-month followup study. *Schizophrenia Bulletin* 16 (1): 147–156.

Heron, J. Woodburn (1957). The pathology of boredom. *Scientific American* 196 (1): pp. 52–56.

Hevesi, Dennis (1991). *The New York Times*, 7/12/91.

Herszenhorn, David (1998). *The New York Times*, 8/29/98.

Holzman, Philip S. (1995). Thought disorders and the fundamental disturbance of schizophrenia. *Schizophrenia, Alfred Benzon Symposium 38*. R. Fog, J. Gerlach, R. Hemmingsen (Eds.). Muksgaard, Copenhagen, 409–17.

Hurvich, Marvin (1991). Annihilation anxiety: An introduction. In *Psychoanalytic Reflections on Current Issues*, ed. H. Siegel. New York: New York University Press.

Johnson, David Read (1984). Representation of the internal world in catatonic schizophrenia. *Psychiatry* 47: 299–314.

Kaiser, Hellmuth (1955). The problem of responsibility in psychotherapy. *Psychiatry* 18: 205–211; also in (1965) *Effective Psychotherapy: The Contribution of Hellmuth Kaiser*, Louis B. Fierman (Ed.). New York: The Free Press.

Khantzian, Edward J., Kurt S. Haliday, William E. McAuliffe (1990). *Addiction and the Vulnerable Self*. New York: Guilford Press.

Kohut, H. (1971). *The Psychology of Self*, New York: International Universities Press.

Lakoff, Robin T. (1977). Women's language. *Language and Style*, X(4): 222–247.

LeBon, Gustave (1896). *The Crowd: A Study of the Popular Mind*. London: Ernest Benn.

Lewin, Kurt (1935). *A Dynamic Theory of Personality*. New York: McGraw-Hill.

Lifton, Robert Jay (1963). *Thought Reform and the Psychology of Totalism: A Study of "Brainwashing" in China*. New York: W. W. Norton.

London, Artur (1971). *The Confession*. New York: Ballantine Books.

McGhie, Andrew, and James Chapman (1961). Disorders of attention and perception in early schizophrenia. *British Journal of Medical Psychology* 34: 103–116.

Martin, Douglas (1990–1991). *The New York Times*, 9/4/91.

Matussek, Paul (1987). Studies in delusional perception. In Cutting and Shepherd (1952). *The Clinical Roots of the Schizophrenia Concept*. Cambridge: Cambridge University Press.

Morice, Rodney, and Ann Delahunty (1996). Frontal/executive impairments in schizophrenia. *Schizophrenia Bulletin* 22 (1): 125–137.

Nunberg, Herman (1948/1961). On the catatonic attack. In *Practice and Theory of Psychoanalysis*. New York: International Universities Press.

Person, Ethel (1986). Manipulativeness in entrepreneurs and psychopaths. In *Unmasking the Psychopath: Antisocial Personality and Related Syndromes*. William H. Reid, Darwin Dorr, John I. Walker, Jack W. Bonner (Eds.). New York: W. W. Norton.

Piaget, Jean (1932). *The Moral Judgment of the Child*. London: Kegan Paul.

Piaget Jean (1981). *Intelligence and Affectivity: Their Relationship During Child Development*. Palo Alto: Annual Reviews.

Podvoll, Edward M. (1990). *The Seduction of Madness*. New York: Harper Collins.

Rapaport, David (1950). On the psychoanalytic theory of thinking. *Collected Papers of David Rapaport*. Merton G. Gill (Ed.). New York: Basic Books, 1967, pp. 313–328.

Rapaport, David (1951). *Organization and Pathology of Thought*. New York: Columbia University Press.

Rapoport, Judith (1989). *The Boy Who Couldn't Stop Washing: The Experience and Treatment of Obsessive-Compulsive Disorder*. New York: Dutton.

Reid, W. H., D. Dorr, J. Walker, and J. W. Bonner (1986). *Unmasking the Psychopath*. New York: Norton.

Rosenbaum, B., and H. Sonne (1986). *The Language of Psychosis*. New York: New York University Press.

Sass, Louis (1992). *Madness and Modernism*. New York: Basic Books.

Sass, Louis (1994). *The Paradoxes of Delusion: Wittgenstein, Schreber and the Schizophrenic Mind*. Ithaca, N.Y.: Cornell University Press.

Schafer, Roy (1954). *Psychoanalytic Interpretation in Rorschach Testing*. New York: Grune and Stratton.

Schafer, Roy (1976). *A New Language for Psychoanalysis*. New Haven, Conn.: Yale University Press.

Schreber, Daniel P. (1955). *Memoirs of My Nervous Illness*. Translated by Ida MacAlpine and Richard A Hunter. London: William Dawson.

Sechehaye, Marguerite (1968). *Autobiography of a Schizophrenic Girl*. New York: New American Library.

Shakow, David (1977). Segmental set: The adaptive process in schizophrenia. *American Psychologist* 32(2): 129–139.

Shapiro, David (1965). *Neurotic Styles*. New York: Basic Books.

Shapiro, David (1981). *Autonomy and Rigid Character*. New York: Basic Books.

Shapiro, David (1989). *Psychotherapy of Neurotic Character*. New York: Basic Books.

Straus, E. W., and R. M. Griffith (1955). Psuedoreversibility of catatonic stupor. *American Journal of Psychiatry* 111:680–685.

Sullivan, Harry Stack (1962). *Schizophrenia as a Human Process*. New York: Norton.

Tahka, Veikko (1993). *Mind and Its Treatment*. Madison, Conn: International Universities Press.

Tausk, Victor (1933). On the origin of the "Influencing Machine" in schizophrenia. *Psychoanalytic Quarterly* 2:519–556.

Vaillant, George E. (1975). Sociopathy as a human process: A viewpoint. *Archives of General Psychiatry* 32: 178–183.

Venables, P. H. (1987). Cognitive and attentional disorders in the development of schizophrenia. In *Search for the Causes of Schizophrenia*. H. Hafner, W. F. Gattaz, and W. Janzarik (Eds.). New York: Springer-Verlag, pp. 203–213.

Waelder, Robert (1960). *Basic Theory of Psychoanalysis*. New York: International Universities Press.

Werner, Heinz (1948). *Comparative Psychology of Mental Development*. Chicago: Follett, 1968.

Wishnie, Howard (1977). *The Impulsive Personality*. New York: Plenum Press.

Wright, Lawrence (1994). *Remembering Satan*. New York: Knopf.

Index